The New Jerusalem

Pleasures Forevermore In God's Eternal City

Harold Eash

Black Forest Press
San Diego, California
August, 2001
First Edition

The New Jerusalem

Pleasures Forevermore
In God's Eternal City

Harold Eash

PUBLISHED IN THE UNITED STATES OF AMERICA
BY
BLACK FOREST PRESS
P.O.Box 6342
Chula Vista, CA 91909-6342
1-800-451-9404

Scripture quotations marked (NIV) are taken from the HOLY BIBLE, NEW INTERNATIONAL VERSION ® (NIV) ® Copyright © 1973, 1978, 1984 by International bible Society. Used by permission of Zondervan Publishing House. All rights reserved.

Verses marked (NKJ) are taken from The New King James Version, copyright© 1979, 1982 by Thomas Nelso, Inc. Publishers. Used by permission.

Verses marked (NAS) are taken from the New American Standard Bible. © 1960, 1962, 1063, 1968, 1971, 1973, 1975, 1977 by The LockmanFoundation. Used by Permission.

The New Berkeley Version in Modern English, (ML) Revised Edition: Copyright 1945, 1959, Copyright © 1969 by The Zondervan Publishing House. All rights reserved including that of translation. Used by Permission.

Verses marked (RSV) Revised Standard Version, Copyright © 1971 by Zondervan Publishing House. Used by Permission.

Verses marked (LB) The Living Bible Copyright© 1971 by Tyndale House Publishers, Wheaton, Illinois 60187 All rights reserved.

Scriptures and quotes are also taken from the (KJ) King James Version.

Cover Design: Dale and Penni Neely

Disclaimer
This document is an original work of the author. It may include reference to information commonly known or freely available to the general public. Any resemblance to other published information is purely coincidental. The author has in no way attempted to use material not of his own origination. Black Forest Press disclaims any association with or responsibility for the ideas, opinions or facts as expressed by the author of this book. No dialog is totally accurate or precise.

Printed in the United States of America
Library of Congress
Cataloging-in-Publication

ISBN: 1-58275-065-3

Copyright © August, 2001 by Harold Eash
ALL RIGHTS RESERVED

Table of Contents

Foreword... i

Prelude vii

PART 1

The Preparation for the New Jerusalem

Chapter 1   Judgment Is Coming................................... 1

Chapter 2   The Judgment Seat Of Christ.......................... 7
Where does a Christian go at death? Who will be judged at the Judgment Seat of Christ? For what will we be judged? What will be the result? When and where will this judgment take place? (Twelve reasons why I believe in the Pre-Tribulation Rapture of the church.)

Chapter 3   The Great White Throne Judgment.................. 25

Chapter 4   The Judgment Of The Heavens And The Earth... 33
The theory of the "Day of the Lord".
The "Canopied Earth" theory.

PART 2

The Presentation of the New Jerusalem

Chapter 5   A Panoramic View Of The New Jerusalem......... 41
It is an eternal city. It is a literal city. (Seven reasons why I believe the N.J. is a literal city.) It is a holy city. It is a beautiful city. (A comparison of the Garden of Eden with the New Jerusalem.) God Himself will be there. All tragedies and trials will be over.

PART 3

The Description of the New Jerusalem

Chapter 6   A Closer Look.. 59
   Its glory. Its size and shape. Its walls and gates. Its street and river. Its temple. Its light.

PART 4

The People of the New Jerusalem

Chapter 7   Who Will Be There?................................. 81
   The Citizens of the New Jerusalem. The Pre-registered. The Overcomers. The Washed. The Visitors to the New Jerusalem.

Chapter 8   What Will We Be Like?............................. 93

Chapter 9   Will We Know Each Other?........................ 99

Chapter 10   What Will We Do?................................. 105
   We will serve Christ in person, face to face, and reign with Him. We will sing and worship God. We will eat and drink. We will rest.

Conclusion... 116

FOREWORD

I'm getting older. How about you? Bad question to start with. Is one's age measured in years or in aches and pains? If one is as old as he feels, my age fluctuates a lot. Sometimes I am a teenager again, but at other times I must be well over a hundred. But rather than be occupied with the signs of old age: baldness, bifocals, bridge, bulge, and bunions, there are better things that should fill our minds. Thoughts concerning our hope. Our future. Heaven. The New Jerusalem. The glories that await us as believers in the Lord Jesus Christ. Yes, and Christ Himself.

I had the privilege of leading the adult Sunday School class at my church, Elim Evangelical Free Church in Puyallup, Washington. We went through a series of lessons on the New Jerusalem, after we had studied the dispensations in the Bible under the leadership of a very fine layman of the church. Though I had taught it before, it meant a lot more to me this time. Perhaps it was because I had more time to spend on the study and preparation of the lessons, and perhaps because I'll soon be heading that way. It is also true that one learns more than the members of the class. It is my prayer that the Lord will use these pages to lift up our eyes to the glories that await us and prepare us for that bright future in the home He is preparing for us.

I wish to thank my wife, Helen, for her help in reading over the manuscript for errors and making the necessary corrections. The book contains some excellent illustrations done by Norma Andreasen, to whom I am very grateful. With heartfelt love I dedicate this book to my many friends who have gone on before and are presently enjoying the pleasures of our heavenly home. Let me name a few. My godly Sunday School teacher, Mrs. Edna Ferguson, who first asked me if I would like to accept Christ as my Savior, is one of these. Then Pastor John H. Blair, who baptized me and later ordained me for the ministry. Of course, my parents, Clarence and Ethel Eash, and my wife's parents, Rev. and Mrs. Arthur Peterson, all of whom are in heaven now. Dr. L.E. Maxwell, founder and first director of Prairie Bible Institute, now College, and my professor of the book of Revelation, has also gone on ahead. And I could name many more who have had a profound influence on my life. "They being dead, yet speak."

Many Bible teachers avoid the book of Revelation due to the difficulties one faces in trying to explain its teachings. In fact, I was in an adult Sunday School class once when this book was mentioned, and the pastor of the church stated that he had not taught this book because of the difficulties involved. The many different interpretations of the book would also tend to make one shy away from it. Yet it is in God's Word for a purpose. In fact, the first of the seven beatitudes in the book of Revelation promises blessing to those who read this prophecy, to those who listen to its teachings, and to those who heed the warnings and admonitions found in its pages, **Revelation. 1:3**. Then again the sixth beatitude also promises blessing to those who heed the words of the prophecy of this book. Seems to me that it would be a good idea to list these seven beatitudes here in the introduction to this marvelous book, as taken from the New American Standard Version.

Revelation 1:3	"Blessed is he who reads and those who hear the words of the prophecy, and heed the things which are written in it; for the time is near."
Revelation 14:13	"Blessed are the dead who die in the Lord from now on!" 'Yes,' says the Spirit, 'that they may rest from their labors, for their deeds follow with them.'"
Revelation 16:15	"Blessed is the one who stays awake and keeps his garments, lest he walk about naked and men see his shame."
Revelation 19:9	"Blessed are those who are invited to the marriage supper of the Lamb."
Revelation 20:6	"Blessed and holy is the one who has a part in the first resurrection; over these the second death has no power, but they will be priests of God and of Christ and will reign with Him for a thousand years."
Revelation 22:7	"Blessed is he who heeds the words of the prophecy of this book."
Revelation 22:14	"Blessed are those who wash their robes, that they may have the right to the tree of life, and may enter by the gates into the city."

God gave this book to our Savior, the Lord Jesus Christ, that He might reveal its teachings, about the things that will shortly come to pass, to His bond-servants (those who have received Him into their lives and submitted gladly to His control), Revelation 1:1. IT IS NOT A CLOSED BOOK. Read about it in Revelation 22:6.

"And he said to me: 'These words are faithful and true'; and the Lord, the God of the spirits of the prophets, sent His angel to show to His bond-servants the things which must shortly take place." **(NAS)**

This prophecy is not to be sealed up, but conversely, is to be revealed and understood. Read it in 22:10.

"And he said to me, 'Do not seal up the words of the prophecy of this book, for the time is near.'" **(NAS)**

Though it is certainly true that it is a difficult book, yet not too difficult for the Holy Spirit to reveal to us those teachings that He wants us to understand and heed. The command to John was just the opposite of the command to Daniel in ***Daniel 12:4*** and ***9***. Here it is.

"But as for you, Daniel, conceal these words and seal up the book until the end of time..."
"And he said, 'Go your way, Daniel, for these words are concealed and sealed up until the end time.'" **(NAS)**

So the book of Revelation is not a closed book; it has not been sealed up; it is meant to be read, understood and heeded. And you will be blessed if you do.

We are blest with many Bibles and many versions of the Bible, so I have used quite a few of these in the Scriptures presented in these pages. These versions, along with their abbreviations, are as follows:

KJ   King James

NKJ New King James

NIV New International Version

LB Living Bible

ML Modern Language

RSV Revised Standard Version

NAS New American Standard

PRELUDE
(Revelation 4 & 5)

The apostle John suddenly saw a door standing open in heaven and heard an angelic voice saying: "Come up here, and I will show you what must take place after these things." What a sight awaited him! The throne of God with four living creatures and 24 elders around it, the book in the hand of God that no one was found worthy to open until the Lamb took the book in His hand, and then the great chorus of praise that went up! What beautiful music he was privileged to hear! It is always a thrill to listen to the music of a great choir, especially when they sing Handel's "Hallelujah Chorus." But no man has ever witnessed nor listened to a more beautiful and awe-inspiring crescendo of praise than the one which followed.

Read it yourself in *Revelation 5:9-14*. The four living creatures and the 24 elders began to pluck their harps and sing a new song to the Lamb:

"Worthy art Thou to take the book, and to break its seals; for Thou wast slain, and didst purchase for God with Thy blood men from every tribe and tongue and people and nation, And Thou hast made them to be a kingdom and priests to our God, and they will reign upon the earth." (NAS)

The choral anthem of praise to God had begun. At this point John looked and heard the voices of thousands of thousands of angels, more than a million angels, around the throne, joining loudly in this great song of praise with these words:

"Worthy is the Lamb that was slain to receive power and riches and wisdom and might and honor and glory and blessing." (NAS)

The four living creatures could not contain their joy, and constantly shouted their "amens". Can you imagine the scene as millions of angelic beings loudly proclaim the praises of the Lamb! Emphasis on the word "loudly". But that was not all. At that moment all of creation joined in the song. God suddenly gave voice to every created thing in heaven, on the earth, under the earth, and in the sea, and altogether they lifted a mighty crescendo of praise with these words:

"To Him who sits on the throne, and to the Lamb, be blessing and honor and glory and dominion forever and ever." (NAS)

Wow! Try to picture the scene in your mind's eye. First the 24 elders and 4 living creatures, then the millions of angels joining in, with the elders shouting their "amen" over and over, and finally all of creation lifting its voice in a mighty anthem of praise to God. Awesome!

"BLESS THE LORD, o my soul, and all that is within me bless His holy name!" (Psalm 103:1 RSV)

What was the occasion of this amazing hymn-sing? The Lamb was about to open the book that He had taken from the hand of His Father. This book would reveal the final judgments of God on this sin-cursed earth, continue with the return of Christ to rule with a rod of iron for a thousand years, and conclude with the beautiful picture of the final home of the redeemed, the New Jerusalem, and the eternity of peace and joy that will unfold. May your reaction to the glories that await you, if you know Christ as your Savior, in some small way parallel the praise and worship around the throne as the book is about to be opened! But before we take a look at the future glory that awaits all of God's children, let's look at the events that lead up to it.

PART 1

THE PREPARATION FOR THE NEW JERUSALEM

The New Jerusalem is referred to as the Holy City. This remarkable statement is made in **Revelation 21:2-3** :

"I saw the Holy City, the new Jerusalem, coming down out of heaven from God, prepared as a bride beautifully dressed for her husband. And I heard a loud voice from the throne, saying: 'Now the dwelling of God is with men, and he will live with them. They will be his people, and God himself will be with them and be their God.'" (NIV)

The city will be holy because God in His absolute holiness will be there. Amazing! *How* can this be? How can a holy God dwell among sinful men in a corrupt and contaminated earth? He can't! Everything has to be changed first. The corruption and contamination caused by sin must be removed. Since God is holy and righteous, there must first be judgment against sin and all that has been defiled.

Chapter One
Judgment Is Coming

The book of Revelation is a book of judgment, judgment against the wicked people of the end times, judgment against the antichrist, the false prophet, and Satan himself, and the final judgment at the great white throne of God. However, since my purpose here is to spotlight the New Jerusalem, and not detail the events of the Great Tribulation, I will limit myself to discussing three judgments that we need to take a look at, because they prepare the way for the City of God and eternity. First. let's look at some verses that warn of coming judgment in general.

"And as it is appointed unto men once to die, but after this the judgment." (Hebrews 9:27 KJ)

"For the time already past is sufficient for you to have carried out the desire of the Gentiles, having pursued a course of sensuality, lusts, drunkenness, carousals, drinking parties, and abominable idolatries. And in all this, they are surprised that you do not run with them into the same excess of dissipation, and they malign you; but they shall give account to Him who is ready to judge the living and the dead." (1 Peter 4:3-5 NAS)

"I charge you therefore before God and the Lord Jesus Christ, who will judge the living and the dead at His appearing and His kingdom." (2 Tim. 4:1 NKJ)

The words "Day of Judgment" appear only six times in the New Testament, but the statement that God will judge appears many more. It is reasonable to expect a day of judgment, since God is righteous in all His acts. Demonized men like Hitler and Stalin must be called to account for their evil deeds. Though some men's judgment comes at least partially in the present time, many people appear to get away with their crimes completely. Yet their day is coming.

The story is told about a man who was walking around a cemetery on his way home, when he suddenly heard voices coming from the cemetery. A high wall around the cemetery kept him from seeing those who were speaking. A couple of boys had climbed the wall and were stealing apples from an apple tree beside the wall. The man stopped and listened to them. They were dividing the apples that they had knocked down. "This one is for you. This one is mine. This is yours. This one is mine." And so they continued until they finished. As the man on the other side of the wall heard this, he concluded that God and Satan were dividing up the souls of the dead. One apple had fallen on the other side of the wall, and so one boy asked: "Who gets the one on the other side of the wall?" Startled and frightened, the man took off running as fast as he could go. He knew that judgment is coming, though he wasn't exactly clear on the details.

An atheist farmer decided he was going to prove that God does not exist. His plan was to do all his work on Sunday in defiance of God's law as he understood it. Surely a righteous God would see this and cause his crop to fail, so he thought. If nothing happened to punish him, then there could not be a God. So he plowed his fields on Sunday, planted his seed on Sunday, and later took in his harvest on Sunday. Lo and behold, he had a bumper crop, the biggest and best harvest of any farmer for miles around. Thinking he had proved his point, he sent a letter to the local newspaper, relating his experiences and stating that this proved there is no God. The editor of the paper, a Christian man, printed the whole letter just as he had received it. After the letter he added these words: "God does not always pay His debts in October!" True. There will come a time when God will hold all accountable for their actions. Those who think they will get away with their unlawful and corrupt practices will find otherwise.

The Bible speaks of four final judgments, five if you take the parable of the sheep and the goats in Matthew 25 as a separate judgment on the nations to determine which ones will enter the millennium. Leaving out this judgment plus the judgments of the Great Tribulation, we will zero in on the remaining three. All of these must take place before the New Jerusalem, the city of God, comes down from heaven to the cleansed earth to become the eternal abode of God's people.

Chapter Two
The Judgment Seat Of Christ

Where does a Christian go at death? Someone has aptly stated that "no one is leaving this planet alive." As one grows older, more and more of his friends pass away and leave this planet. We know the body goes into a grave, unless the corpse has been cremated. Two friends of mine had their ashes scattered across a lake they loved. But what about their spirit and soul? Where is the real person, the one who lived within that house we call a body? God's Word is very clear on this point. Those who have received Christ as Savior have experienced a new birth, a spiritual birth, and have Christ's own promise that their life is eternal. The expression "eternal life" carries with it two meanings: duration of time - time never ceasing, and quality of time - an abundant and joyful life in Christ. Death is simply a transition from this earthly existence to a far better heavenly home. Let me share a few favorite Scriptures with you.

"For to me, to live is Christ, and to die is gain. But if I am to live on in the flesh, this will mean fruitful labor for me; and I do not know which to choose. But I am hard-pressed from both directions, having the desire to depart and be with Christ, for that is very much better." (Phil. 1:21-23 NAS)

"For we know that if the earthly tent which is our house is torn down, we have a building from God, a house not made with hands, eternal

in the heavens. Therefore, being always of good courage, and knowing that while we are at home in the body we are absent from the Lord-for we walk by faith, not by sight-we are of good courage, I say, and prefer rather to be absent from the body and to be at home with the Lord." (2 Cor. 5:1, 6-8 NAS)

What a glorious future will be ours! As the song written many years ago promises: "We'll say goodnight here, but good morning up there." There will be no intermediate state. When Scripture refers to a dead Christian as being asleep, it means that his body is asleep, awaiting the resurrection. But the soul and spirit have gone directly into the presence of God to enjoy the blessings of that heavenly home. We have no need to fear death as it is just a step to glory. Today Paradise is in heaven where those who died in Christ are enjoying the fellowship of Christ's presence. A funeral service I attended inspired me to write the following lines to be read after my death.

I'VE GONE ON AHEAD

*O what peace and what joy are unceasingly mine,
Since I've reached my glorious home.
In the presence of Jesus, my Savior Divine,
From here I will nevermore roam.*

*Such melodious songs that the angels intone,
For those who have been reconciled!
And those joyous words forever will ring,
"Welcome to Heaven, my Child!"*

*Don't weep for me, for my pain passed away,
When the angel God sent lifted me.*

And His peace filled my heart as homeward I flew
Toward that glorious light I could see.

I know it was hard to bid me goodbye,
But remember it's just for awhile
I've gone on ahead to wait for you here.
I'll welcome you home with a smile.

I wish you God's best in the days still ahead
So be faithful and true to the Lord.
'Till I meet you up here in this wonderful place,
Where life over death is restored.

I'm hungry no more, for His Word is my food,
And thirst I will never more know.
All sickness and pain have vanished away,
No sadness like down there below.

I've entered my rest, eternal and sweet,
I'm living far more than before.
So hurry along and meet me up here.
I'll wait on this beautiful shore.

When we reach heaven, it will be a place of joy and rest, but there will also be judgment.

Who will be judged at this time?

The apostle Peter refers to this judgment in ***1 Peter 4:17-18*** when he states:

"For the time has come for judgment to begin with God's household; and if it starts with us, what will be the destiny of those who disobey the good news from God? And if the righteous person is saved with difficulty, what chance have the impious and sinful?" (ML)

Though the immediate context has to do with suffering for Christ, and this suffering could be taken as the judgment of God, which begins with the church, yet the references to the destiny of those who disobey and the salvation of the righteous clearly point to a future judgment which will begin with the church. The church is first to be judged since the family must give account before those who are outside. Now let's look at the two principal passages of Scripture that tell us of the judgment of believers.

"For we must all appear before the judgment seat of Christ, that each one may receive what is due him for the things done while in the body, whether good or bad." (2 Corinthians 5:10 NIV)

"Why do you pass judgment on your brother? Or you, why do you despise your brother? For we shall all stand before the judgment seat of God; for it is written: 'As I live, says the Lord, every knee shall bow to me, and every tongue shall give praise to God.' So each of us shall give account of himself to God." (Romans 14:10-12 RSV)

The judgment seat of Christ is the judgment seat of God, since Christ is God the Son. That He will be the judge is clearly stated in *John 5:22, 26-27:*

"Moreover, the Father judges no one, but has entrusted all judgment to the Son... For as the Father has life in himself, so he has granted the Son to have life in himself. And he has given him authority to judge, because he is the Son of Man." (NIV)

For what will we be judged?

Judgment will take place on "the things done while in the body, whether good or bad", according to the apostle Paul in his Corinthian letter. To the Romans he states that every born-again believer will give account of himself to God. Thus every true Christian will give an account to God about the good and the bad things he or she did while living in this mortal body. But let's be more specific. To what is he referring? Undoubtedly the most complete passage along this line is found in *1 Corinthians 3:11-15*. It states:

"And no one can ever lay any other real foundation than the one we already have - Jesus Christ. But there are various kinds of materials that can be used to build on that foundation. Some use gold and silver and jewels; and some build with sticks, and hay, or even straw! There is going to come a time of testing at Christ's Judgment Day to see what kind of material each builder has used. Everyone's work will be put through the fire so that all can see whether or not it keeps its value, and what was really accomplished. Then every workman who has built on the foundation with the right materials, and whose work still stands, will get his pay. But if the house he has built burns up, he will have a great loss. He himself will be saved, but like a man escaping through a wall of flames." (LB)

Salvation is not the issue at this judgment. It is not our sin, but our works that will be judged. What have we done for Christ? What have we done to advance His kingdom? What have we done for others? How have we built upon the foundation of our faith, Jesus Christ? What pay (reward) will we get? This is what it's all about. God loves us and has a wonderful plan for our lives. How have you fit into His plan?

Another verse that bears on this subject is *1 Corinthians 4:5*. It reads:

"Therefore judge nothing before the time, until the Lord comes, who will both bring to light the hidden things of darkness and reveal the counsels of the hearts. Then each one's praise will come from God."   *(NKJ)*

That the judgment will be complete and perfect is seen by the fact that all of the things which have been kept secret, either knowingly or unknowingly, including the thoughts and reasonings behind our actions, will be openly manifested, and taken into consideration in the judgment. God does not judge according to the outward appearance but according to the heart. Then those who have served the Lord with pure motives for His glory will receive praise from Him. Can you imagine what it will be like to be praised by God Almighty Himself?

Yes, we will be judged for our works. However, salvation is not by works but by grace alone through faith in the finished work of Christ on the Cross. But then works should follow as a result of our salvation experience. *Ephesians 2:8-10* puts this in the right perspective with these words:

"For by grace you have been saved through faith; and this is not your own doing, it is the gift of God - not because of works, lest any man should boast. For we are his workmanship, created in Christ Jesus for good works, which God prepared beforehand, that we should walk in them." (RSV)

A good life filled with good deeds will never earn us salvation, since Christ did this once for all when he died in our place on the Cross, but after we become his children, He expects us to do the works that He has planned for us.

I had the privilege of attending Prairie Bible Institute (now College) for four good years, and often heard Dr. L.E. Maxwell quote a favorite little poem of his. I have no idea who wrote these lines, but the poet did an excellent job of defining salvation without works. It goes like this.

There is nothing to do, for being born dead,
You must have another to work in your stead.
Christ Jesus in Calvary's terrible hour,
Has done all the work in such marvelous power,
That, raised from the dead, He now offers to you
Life, pardon, salvation; and nothing to do.
No, nothing to do 'til you're saved from your sins,
When the power of doing good only begins.

As believers in Christ, born again by the Holy Spirit, we will never be judged for our sin. Why? Because Christ was judged for it on the Cross. We have been forgiven, and made perfect in Christ, **Hebrews 10:14**. God has cast our sins into the depths of the sea, **Micah 7:19**. And, as someone has aptly stated, He then put up a "No Fishing" sign. He blots out all our sins and remembers them no more, **Isaiah 43:25**. Our epitaph could well be the one word "forgiven", as in the following poem by an unknown author, simply entitled:

Forgiven

Not far from New York, in a cemetery lone,
Close guarding its grave, stands a simple headstone,
And all the inscription is one word alone - "Forgiven."

No sculptor's fine art has embellished its form,
But constantly there through the calm and the storm,
It beareth this word from a poor fallen worm - "Forgiven."

It shows not the date of the silent one's birth,
Reveals not his frailties, nor lies of his worth,
But speaks out this tale from his few feet of earth - "Forgiven."
The date is unmentioned, the name is untold.
Beneath lies the body, corrupted and cold,
Above rests his spirit, at home in the fold - "Forgiven."

And when, from the heavens, the Lord shall descend,
This stranger shall rise, and to glory ascend,
Well known and befriended, to sing without end - "Forgiven."

What will be the result of the judgment of the value of our works?

According to **1 Corinthians 3:11-15** each believer's work will be tested, with two possible results:

First, some believers will suffer loss, when their work is totally burned up. It must be about this possibility that John writes:

"And now, little children, abide in him, so that when he appears, we may have confidence and not shrink from him in shame at his coming." **(1 John 2:28 RSV)**

But what is this fire of judgment that burns up the wood, hay, and stubble? Is this a figurative fire or a real one? An indication is given in **Revelation 1:14** in the description of the Son of God Himself as He walks among the churches. It states:

"His head and hair were white like wool, as white as snow, and his eyes were like blazing fire." (NIV)

Could Paul be talking about the fiery, penetrating, all-seeing eyes of Christ as He sits in judgment of each one's works? What an awesome and fearful thought! The question of great importance to all who desire above everything to be pleasing to Him and have works that remain is this. What are the works that will be burned up? Without going into detail here, Scripture makes it clear that those who serve Christ for their own glory have their reward, **Matthew 6:1-5, 16-18**. The praise of men. Their works will be burned up. Like the man who approached his pastor and asked if he could sing a solo. The pastor agreed and invited him to come back on Wednesday for the mid-week prayer meeting to sing his solo. "But," he protested. "I want to sing it on Sunday morning." Did he want to sing for the glory of God, or for his own glory? On the other hand I have heard it said: "We haven't practiced this song, but we are going to do it for the glory of God." Does God deserve something poorly done? Certainly not! We should do our very best for Him, and do it for His glory.

Those things that are done in the flesh and not in the Spirit will also be worthless in that day, **Galatians 6:7-8**. There will be no reward for such activities, for "the flesh profiteth nothing." Take a moment to reflect on your service for Christ. Do you teach, or preach, or serve in other capacities, so that people will think well of you, and congratulate you on a job well done? Are you working hard for the Lord in all the energy that your flesh can produce? If so, your work will burn up. No reward! None at all! Or are you resting in Christ and the Holy Spirit to empower you, and giving all the glory to Him? This work will remain and be rewarded.

That brings us to the second result, that, just as some believers will suffer loss and receive no rewards, other believers work will be rewarded. Just like there will be some who will shrink away from Christ ashamed on that day, so others will be confident. This possibility is expressed by the apostle John in **1 John 4:17**.

"In this way, love is made complete among us so that we will have confidence on the day of

judgment, because in this world we are like him." (NIV)

There are quite a few verses that promise rewards for faithful service. You can look up on your own *2 John 8, Matthew 10:42, Luke 6:35, Colossians 3:23-25,* and *Ephesians 6:7-8,* to name a few. The words of the apostle Paul in *Philippians 4:16-17* should be an encouragement to every giver to the Lord's work. Listen to his promise:

"For even when I was in Thessalonica you sent me aid again and again when I was in need. Not that I am looking for a gift, but I am looking for what may be credited to your account." (NIV)

This sacrificial giving of the Philippian believers was credited to their account. Where was this account kept? I doubt very much that Paul himself was keeping the account, though he did remember their giving. He must be referring to a heavenly accounting that will someday produce rewards for the givers. Those of us who have had the privilege to serve the Lord in missionary work and those who are presently serving the Lord as missionaries are deeply indebted to a great host of fellow Christians without whose financial and prayer support our ministry would not have been the same. All of this gets credited to their account. Let me tell you about one of these givers.

After every four years of ministry in Venezuela, my wife and I and our three sons would come home on furlough, now called home assignment. Besides the normal housing and transportation needs, we also would be in need of a new wardrobe. There was a dear lady in my home church, Llanerch Hills Chapel of Upper Darby, Pa., who immediately reached out to us. Dorothy Graham would approach us at one of the first meetings we attended to invite us to go with her to the 69th Street shopping center. What a time we had! Aunt Dorothy would take us to Lit Brothers and outfit us. There were trousers and shirts for the boys and for me. A dress, a skirt and a blouse for Helen. Then shoes and socks for all of us. And of course, she had to stop at the candy department. Then when our shopping was done, she would take us to a local restaurant for Philly steak and cheese sandwiches. Delicious! Do you think we enjoyed these times? You can bet we did. But you should have seen Aunt Dorothy. I'm sure she got as much fun out of spending her money to provide for us as we did from receiving it. All this has been added to her account, and she is now in the presence of God and enjoying the glories of heaven.

Five crowns are mentioned as rewards for different reasons. They are as follows:

1. The incorruptible crown or imperishable wreath of **1 Corinthians 9:25**.
2. The crown of rejoicing from **1 Thessalonians 2:19**.
3. The crown of righteousness in **2 Timothy 4:7-8**.
4. The crown of life from **James 1:12** and **Revelation 2:10**.
5. The unfading crown of glory of **1 Peter 5:1-4**.

I was teaching this on one occasion when a member of the class stated that this was difficult for him to understand, because none of us merits a crown from Christ. How true! When we have done our best, we should consider that we are still unprofitable servants. We have this on good authority, that of Christ Himself. Why do we get the crowns and what will we do with them? Are they real crowns or just symbolic? We do not know the answers to many of these questions. If real crowns, I like to think that we will do with them as the 24 elders in **Revelation 4:10** who laid their crowns before the throne in an act of worship and praise. When I mentioned this to the brother who was having a hard time with the idea of getting crowns, he was satisfied.

It was the thought of standing before Christ at this judgment that inspired the writing of an anonymous poem, entitled:

His Plan for Me

When I stand at the judgment seat of Christ,
And He shows me His plan for me;
The plan of my life as it might have been
Had He had His way, and I see
How I blocked Him here and checked Him there,
And I would not yield my will;
Will there be grief in my Savior's eyes,
Grief, though He loves me still?

He would have me rich, and I stand there poor,
Stripped of all but His grace,
While memory runs like a hunted thing
Down the paths I cannot retrace.
Then my desolate heart will well-nigh break
With the tears that I cannot shed!
I shall cover my face with my empty hands.
I shall bow my uncrowned head.
Lord of the years that are left to me,
I give them to Thy hand.
Take me, and break me, and mold me
To the pattern that Thou hast planned.

When and where will this judgment take place?

Though it is not clearly spelled out in Scripture, there are many indications that the judgment seat of Christ will take place at the end of the age of grace, during the last 7 years before the beginning of the thousand year reign of Christ. Some consider this whole period to be the time of the Great Tribulation. Others feel that only the last 3 1/2 years qualifies for this title. There are also many views as to the time of the return of Christ. Will he come before the Great Tribulation, in the middle of it, or at the close? For the judgment seat of Christ to take place in heaven during the Great Tribulation here on earth, the rapture of the church must come before the Great Tribulation. Let me give you a number of reasons why I believe this to be true.

WHY I BELIEVE IN THE PRE-TRIBULATION RAPTURE OF THE CHURCH.

1. Christ's Coming is imminent. We are told to watch and wait and be ready. If the rapture takes place after the Great Tribulation, or even in the middle of it, the church would be watching for the Antichrist and the Great Tribulation instead of watching for Christ. The New Testament writers expected Him at any time, **Philippians 4:5, James 5:8, 1 Peter 4:7, 1 John 2:18**. If His coming is to be delayed until after or during the Great Tribulation, this would be little comfort to the church, **1 Thessalonians 4:18**. The exhortation to purify ourselves in view of His coming has the most significance if His coming is imminent, **1 John 3:2-3**.

An eminent visitor to a grade school greatly impressed the children there. Before he left. he promised to return, but could not tell them when. He stated that upon his return, he would give a prize to the boy or girl with the cleanest desk. One little girl stated that she was going to win that prize. The other children laughed, as hers was the dirtiest desk in the room. She declared that everyday before going home she would clean up her desk. "But what if he comes before school is out?" asked another child. "Well, I'll clean up my desk every day at noon, then," came the reply. "But what if he comes in the morning?" another questioned. "I know what I'll do," answered the little girl. "I'll just keep it clean." And what about you? Don't count on a late opportunity to get ready for His coming. Keep yourself ready.

2. The Great Tribulation is the time of God's wrath, Revelation *6:16-17, 11:18, 15:1, 16:1*. The church is to be delivered from this wrath, *1 Thessalonians 1:10* and *5:9*.

3. At the rapture, the church will be taken to heaven to the home that Christ is now preparing, *John 14:1-3*. According to *13:36, Peter*, possibly representing the church, will follow Christ to where He was going, namely to heaven.

It is beautiful how this teaching fulfills the Jewish marriage customs of that day, where the groom went to the house of the bride, and took her back to his father's house. The presence of the church in heaven during the time of the Great Tribulation on earth provides time for the Judgment Seat of Christ and the Marriage Supper of the Lamb before the Millennium begins. It should be noted that before the Great Tribulation ends with the

Battle of Armageddon, prepared for in *Revelation 16:13-16*, but actually described in *Revelation 19:11-21*, it is stated in 19:7 that the marriage of the Lamb had come and "His bride has made herself ready." The bride of Christ is the church. When did she make herself ready? Since she was ready before the Great Tribulation ended, then during that time she was evidently preparing herself at the Judgment Seat of Christ.

4. Twice in *2 Thessalonians 2* the Rapture of the Church is said to take place before the Antichrist appears and the Great Tribulation begins. First, in the departure of vs. 3, the word "apostasy" literally means "departure" and is so used in eight of the ten New Testament references that use this Greek word. E. Schuyler and Kenneth Wuest, two of God's choice saints and New Testament authorities, refer this to the rapture of the church. Though we cannot speak with absolute certainty, it seems highly possible that they are right in that the departure referred to is not a departure from the faith, but the departure of the faithful at the rapture of the church. It is clearly stated that this departure will take place before the Day of the Lord, which would be before the Great Tribulation. Second, in vss. 6-8, in the "taking out of the way" of "he who now restrains". This appears to be a reference to the Holy Spirit being removed in His present day function. Since He indwells the church, the church would be removed at the same time, again before the Day of the Lord.

5. The Great Tribulation is properly interpreted by Pre-tribulationists as the time of Israel's judgment in preparation for all Israel to be saved, *Romans 11:26*. It

is Daniel's 70th week, ***Daniel 9:24-27***. All 70 of the weeks mentioned in this passage have to do with Israel. The church is not mentioned there, nor in any New Testament passage, as being in the Great Tribulation.

6. Mid-tribulationists believe that the rapture will occur during the seventh trumpet in Revelation 11 which they take to be the "last trump." However it appears that the second 3 1/2 year period, the middle of the Great Tribulation, begins long before that way back in chapter 6. For the rapture to take place at the seventh trumpet, the church would have to go through a part of the "wrath of God". The last trumpet of ***1 Corinthians 15:52*** is not the seventh or last of the trumpet judgments. It is the last trumpet of the church age, calling God's people together for the rapture. The seven trumpet judgments of the book of Revelation belong to a separate series of trumpets, and have nothing to do with the church.

7. The possible interpretation of ***Matthew 24:38-41*** as being the rapture when some are taken out while others are left, before the Great Tribulation, speaks of a pre-trib rapture. This may not be the correct interpretation of this passage, but the other view, that those who were taken out were taken in judgment, has its difficulties, so I would not rule the rapture out of this passage.

8. Revelation 7 is an amazing interlude between the sixth and seventh seals. The Great Tribulation is underway. The Antichrist has appeared to conquer the earth, war breaks out, followed by famine and death. Then the martyrs cry to God for justice, at which God responds by shaking the earth and opening the heavens to reveal His throne. So fearsome is the scene that the

people hide in the caves and call for the rocks to fall on them. The sixth seal has passed.

Now before going on to the 7th, and direct judgments from God as His wrath is poured out, it is necessary to seal those Jewish believers, 12,000 from each of the 12 tribes, who are to be kept safe, perhaps to take the Gospel to the world. But where is the church? Why are the members of the church of Christ not sealed also? Where are they? They are already raptured and enjoying heaven's glories.

The scene in ***Revelation 7:9-17*** pictures the church in heaven toward the start of the Great Tribulation and having escaped it. It is a great multitude that no man can count from all tribes and tongues and peoples and nations of the earth. Could such a vast multitude be saved during the short time of the Great Tribulation? If so, to be in heaven they would have had to either die a natural death or be martyred. Notice also that this heavenly scene takes place toward the beginning of the Great Tribulation. It is highly unlikely, though not impossible, that such a vast multitude from every nation on earth could have been saved and then die a natural death or be martyred for their faith in just a year or two of time. Verse 14 describes them as having come out of the Great Tribulation. This could also be translated "away from", as in ***Revelation 3:10***, where the church in Philadelphia is promised that it will be kept from (away from) the hour of testing (a reference to the G.T.). Notice that it is to be kept "from" not "through" the hour of testing. The church does not come "out of" the Great Tribulation, as some translations have it, but "away from", having left before it started.

9. The rapture of the church is pre-pictured in previous deliverances. Just as Noah was delivered before the rains fell and the flood came, and just as Lot

was taken out of Sodom before its destruction, so God will take out the church before the G.T. begins.

10. That the Rapture and the Second Coming are two distinct events, not one and the same as the post-trib teachers believe, is evident in Scripture. At the Rapture Christ meets the saints in the air, *1 Thessalonians 4:16-17*, while at the Second Coming He returns to the Mount of Olives to meet the few saints of that day on earth, *Zechariah 14:1-4*. It is interesting that Christ left this earth from the Mount of Olives, *Acts 1:9-12*, and will return at the close of the G.T. to the Mount of Olives.

The Rapture is described as imminent, with no unfulfilled prophecy holding it up, while there are definite signs for the Second Coming.

11. Scripture pictures a time of peace and prosperity before the Rapture, *Matthew 24:37-39, 1 Thessalonians 5:2-3*. This could hardly describe the conditions at the end of the Great Tribulation with its devastation and destruction as recorded in the book of Revelation.

12. Christ asked the question: "When the Son of Man comes, will He find faith on the earth?" *(Luke 18:8)* The negative answer that this question requires cannot be applied to His coming for the church at the Rapture, since at that time, He will certainly find faith on the earth. The true Christians of that glorious day, having been saved by faith, will be awaiting Him. This must be applied to His Second Coming at the end of the G.T., after the believers of that time are martyred for their faith, *Revelation 13:15-17, 20:4*. Evidently at that time, *Revelation 1:7-9*, all Israel of that day will be saved, *Romans 11:26*.

Chapter Three
The Great White Throne Judgment

Let me quote the writer of the book to the Hebrews when he states:

"And inasmuch as it is appointed for men to die once, and after this comes judgment." (Hebrews 9:27 NAS)

One of the most powerful motives to turn men to God is the fear of the coming judgment. It should be shouted from the pulpit. God will judge the world! No escaping it! The day is coming!

The story is told of an infidel who attempted to engage a preacher in a debate at the close of a church service. The preacher refused to be drawn into the argument, stating simply that the Bible says: "It is appointed unto men once to die, and after this the judgment." The agnostic insisted, but again heard the same Scripture quoted. This happened a number of times, until the man became angry and stalked off. On the way home that verse kept running through his mind. The wind blowing through the trees seemed to whisper "judgment". The water in the brook under the bridge he crossed seemed to murmur "judgment, judgment". The next morning the pastor was awakened early by a knock on his door. It was the agnostic. He blurted out to the pastor that he could not sleep as that word "judgment" kept coming back and haunting him. Right there he made his peace with God.

An unknown poet penned the following lines on this theme. It's entitled:

What then?

When the great plants of our cities
Have turned out their last finished work;
When our merchants have sold their last yard of silk,
And dismissed the last tired clerk.
When our banks have taken in their last dollar,
And paid the last dividend;
When the judge of the earth says: "Closed for the night,"
And asks for a balance - what then?

When the choir has sung its last anthem,
And the preacher has made his last prayer.
When the people have heard their last sermon,
Ant the sound has died out in the air;
When the Bible lies closed on the altar,
And the pews are all empty of men;
And each one stands facing his record,
And the great book is opened - what then?

When the actors have played their last drama,
And the mimic has made his last fun;
When the film has flashed its last picture,
And the billboard displayed its last run;
When the crowds seeking pleasure have vanished,
And gone out into the darkness again;
When the trumpet of ages is sounded,
And we stand up before Him - what then?

When the bugle's call sinks into silence,
And the long marching columns stand still;
When the captain repeats his last orders,
And they've captured the last fort and hill,
And the flag has been hauled from the masthead,
And the wounded afield checked in,
And the world that rejected its Savior,
Is asked for a reason, what then?

What an awesome day that will be! True, it won't happen exactly as the poet wrote it, since the judgment of the unsaved will not take place until the end of the Millennium, yet this should in no way decrease the seriousness of coming judgment. The major passage that explains what will happen at that time is **Revelation 20:11-15**.

"And I saw a great white throne and the one who sat upon it, from whose face the earth and sky fled away, but they found no place to hide. I saw the dead, great and small, standing before God; and The Books were opened, including the Book of Life. And the dead were judged according to the things written in The Books, each according to the deeds he had done. The oceans surrendered the bodies buried in them; and the earth and the underworld gave up the dead in them. Each was judged according to his deeds. And Death and Hell were thrown into the Lake of Fire. This is the Second Death - the Lake of Fire. And if anyone's name was not found recorded in the Book of Life, he was thrown into the Lake of Fire." (LB)

John saw a great white throne in heaven and one seated on the throne. We have already noted from **John 5:22 and 27** that the Father is not the judge but has given all judgment to the Son. Who are being judged? The dead, small and great. Since the judgment Seat of Christ has already taken place and the church has been judged, Christians are not the object of this judgment, though it would appear that they are present. Two other Bible verses bear upon this subject directly.

"On the day when, according to my Gospel, God will judge the secrets of men through Christ Jesus." (Romans 2:16 NAS)

> *"And I say to you, that every careless word that men shall speak, they shall render account for it in the day of judgment."* (Matt. 12:36 NAS)

The Revelation description of this historic event clearly states that each one will be judged according to his works. Christ adds that even his words will be taken into account. But where will the evidence come from? God's Books. His own personal library. The Negro spiritual says it well: *"He sees all that you do, and He hears all that you say. My Lord is writin' all the time."*

These Books are history books or scrolls with the works of every one written in them. Since the judgment will be according to the conduct of each one, his works and words, there will evidently be degrees of punishment. Other Scriptures add another dimension to this by teaching that the light one has received will also be taken into consideration. For instance:

> *"Much is required from them to whom much is given, for their responsibility is greater."* (Luke 12:48b LB)

> *"Then He began to reproach the cities in which most of His miracles were done, because they did not repent. "Woe to you, Chorazin! Woe to you, Bethsaida! For if the miracles had occurred in Tyre and Sidon which occurred in you, they would have repented long ago in sackcloth and ashes. Nevertheless I say to you, it shall be more tolerable for Tyre and Sidon in the day of judgment, than for you. And you, Capernaum, will not be exalted to heaven, will you? You shall descend to Hades, for if the miracles had occurred in Sodom which occurred in you, it would have remained to this day. Nevertheless I say to you that it shall*

be more tolerable for the land of Sodom in the day of judgment, than for you." (Matthew 11:20-24 NAS)

"For if we go on sinning willfully after receiving the knowledge of the truth, there no longer remains a sacrifice for sins, but a certain terrifying expectation of judgment, and the fury of a fire which will consume the adversaries." (Hebrews 10:26-27 NAS)

The Book of Life plays a very important part in the condemnation of the unsaved. Before judgment is carried out on an individual, a check is made in the Book of Life to locate his name. If it is not recorded there, he is then cast into the Lake of Fire. God not only keeps a record of the works of each one, but He especially takes careful note of all those who accept Christ as Savior, and has their name inscribed in the Book of Life. There are eight verses in the Bible that mention or at least refer to the Book of Life. Let me list them for you.

"Now at that time Michael, the great prince who stands guard over the sons of your people, will arise. And there will be a time of distress such as never occurred since there was a nation until that time; and at that time, your people, everyone who is found written in the book, will be rescued." (Daniel 12:1 NAS)

"Nevertheless do not rejoice in this, that the spirits are subject to you, but rejoice that your names are recorded in heaven." (Luke 10:20 NAS)

"Indeed, true comrade, I ask you to help these women who have shared my struggle in the cause of the gospel, together with Clement also, and the rest of my fellow-workers, whose names are in the book of life." (Phil. 4:3 NAS)

> *"...to the general assembly and church of the first-born who are enrolled in heaven, and to God the Judge of all, and to the spirits of righteous men made perfect." (Hebrews 12:23 NAS)*
>
> *"He who overcomes shall thus be clothed in white garments; and I will not erase his name from the book of life, and I will confess his name before My Father, and before His angels." (Revelation 3:5 NAS)*
>
> *"And all who dwell on the earth will worship him, every one whose name has not been written from the foundation of the world in the book of life of the Lamb who has been slain." (Revelation 13:8 NAS)*
>
> *"And if anyone's name was not found written in the book of life, he was thrown into the lake of fire." (Revelation 20:15 NAS)*
>
> *"And nothing unclean and no one who practices abomination and lying, shall ever come into it, but only those whose names are written in the Lamb's book of life." (Revelation 21:27 NAS)*

Is your name written in that book? Your eternal salvation depends upon it. If you are not sure, lift your heart to God in prayer and tell Him that you want Christ to be your Savior, that you are sorry for your sin, and turn your life over to Him. You'll be born again, forgiven of your sin, and your name will be recorded in heaven.

Those whose names are not recorded in the Book of Life are cast into the Lake of Fire. This is the eternal destination of the unsaved. They will not be alone there, because previously the Beast and the False Prophet and Satan himself will be cast there,

Revelation 20:10, but this will certainly be no consolation to them. There is a hell and a heaven, but neither are eternal destinies. Those without Christ go to hell, called Hades in Greek, awaiting the day of judgment. Then they are cast into the Lake of Fire. Christians go to heaven at death, but only temporarily. Their eternal abode is the New Jerusalem on earth.

Hell, or Hades, is also cast into the Lake of Fire along with death. These two are like twin personalized demons, death being the door to eternity, the grave where the bodies are kept, and hell (Hades) being the underworld abode of spirits of the unsaved until judgment day. These two appear together also in ***Revelation 1:17-18 and 6:7-8***. And the last enemy to be destroyed is death itself, according to ***1 Corinthians 15:26***.

The question is sometimes asked by skeptics: "Where is hell?" I love the answer that was given to just such a sneering skeptic during an outdoor meeting: "Hell, my friend, is at the end of a Christless life."

It seems true that Hades originally had two compartments, one for believers and one for unbelievers. Luke 16 talks about Abraham's bosom to which Lazarus went. To this compartment all those who would be saved descended in the hour of death. The rich man was also in Hades, but in another section where the fires of hell inflicted great torment on its occupants. He could see Lazarus a great way off on the other side of a wide chasm. Yes, Lazarus and the Old Testament saints were also in Hades, though not in torments. However, when Christ ascended on high, he took with Him the whole company of the saved, those who had been held captive in Hades. This is the teaching of ***Ephesians 4:8***.

"This is why it says: 'When he ascended on high, he led captives in his train and gave gifts to men.'" (NIV)

Who were these captives? Those saints of God who had been held captive in Hades awaiting that day. Today Paradise is in heaven, as we have pointed out earlier. But the unsaved still wait in Hades for the day of resurrection and final judgment. What a terrible future awaits them! Those of us who know Christ and have the blessed hope of eternity with Him must do what we can to rescue those who are destined for a Christless eternity.

Chapter Four
The Judgment Of The Heavens And The Earth

There are two Old Testament prophecies concerning this event in the book of Isaiah.

"Behold, I will create new heavens and a new earth. The former things will not be remembered, nor will they come to mind." (65:17 NIV)

"'As the new heavens and the new earth that I make will endure before me,' declares the Lord, 'so will your name and descendants endure.'" (66:22 NIV)

And Christ himself promised this would happen in *Matthew 24:35*.

"Heaven and earth will pass away, but my words will never pass away." (NIV)

This cataclysmic event of the destruction of the heavens and the earth is the judgment described in *Revelation 20:11 and 21:1*. It reads as follow:

"Then I saw a great white throne and One seated upon it, from whose presence earth and heaven fled, and no room was found for them."(ML)

"Then I saw a new heaven and a new earth; for the first heaven and the first earth had passed away, and no longer was there any sea." (ML)

The day will come in God's calendar when the present heaven and earth will be done away with. The question arises about how new the new heavens and the new earth will be? Is God going to totally destroy and eradicate all traces of the old, and make a totally new creation? In the Greek in which the New Testament was written, there are two words for "new". The first word "neos" means totally new or "brand new", as we would say today. The other word is "kainos", which means "renewed", made over, changed. The word used here in the book of Revelation is the word "kainos". The earth will be renewed. As someone has stated there will be "fresh life rising from the decay and wreck of the old world."

The question naturally comes as to when this cataclysmic event will take place. There appears to be only one possible time for this to happen, when the earth is emptied of its people, and that is during the great white throne judgment. This is where John places it in Revelation 20:11. While all people of all ages stand before the awesome presence of God Almighty and His Son on that great judgment day, a terrible destruction will take place here on earth and in the sky above. How will God bring about this destruction? We must look to the apostle Peter for the answer to this question.

"But the day of the Lord will come like a thief, in which the heavens will pass away with a roar and the elements will be destroyed with intense heat, and the earth and its works will be burned up. Since all these things are to be destroyed in this way, what sort of people ought you to be in holy conduct and godliness, looking for and hastening the coming of the day of God, on account of which the heavens will be destroyed by burning, and the elements will melt with intense heat! But according to His promise we are looking for new heavens and a new

earth, in which righteousness dwells. (2 Peter 3:10-13 NAS)

But why must the earth be burned up? Take a look at the following verses.

"To Adam he said, 'Because you listened to your wife and ate from the tree about which I commanded you, 'You must not eat of it,' cursed is the ground because of you; through painful toil you will eat of it all the days of your life. It will produce thorns and thistles for you." (Genesis 3:17-18a NIV)

"For on that day thorns and thistles, sin, death, and decay - the things that overcame the world against its will at God's command - will all disappear, and the world around us will share in the glorious freedom from sin which God's children enjoy. For we know that even the things of nature, like animals and plants, suffer in sickness and death as they await this great event." (Romans 8:20-22 LB)

"And there shall no longer be any curse..." (Revelation 22:3 NAS)

This earth is under a curse, the curse of sin, since the day that Adam and Eve disobeyed God and ate from the forbidden fruit. Its destruction is the only answer. The pollution of our land and sea requires such a drastic measure by God. There cannot be any curse in the new earth, for righteousness will totally envelope it.

What about the heavens? Why must they be burned up too? Scripture mentions three heavens, *2 Corinthians 12:1-4*. The atmosphere above us, the starry expanse with myriads of lights and known and unknown planets, and the third heaven, where God has his throne. The first two need to be cleansed, because they have been utterly contaminated. Not only by the space debris and satellites that man has sent there, but even more by the presence of evil spirits. Take a look at the following verses.

"As for you, you were dead in your transgressions and sins, in which you used to live when you followed the ways of this world and of the ruler of the kingdom of the air, the spirit who is now at work in those who are disobedient." (Ephesians 2:1-2 NIV)

"But our struggle is not against flesh and blood, but against the rulers, against the authorities, against the powers of this dark world and against the spiritual forces of evil in the heavenly realms." (Ephesians 6:12 NIV)

Satan, the god of this world, has his base of operations in the heavens. Thus they have been severely contaminated. A day will come when God says, "enough!", and has Satan thrown out of the heavenly realms and down to earth. This is described in detail in **Revelation 12:7-12**.

There are two theories that I would like to briefly mention before getting into the actual presentation of the New Jerusalem in Revelation 21.

The theory of the "day of the Lord"

"For you yourselves know well that the day of the Lord will come like a thief in the night." (1 Thessalonians 5:2 RSV)

God created everything in just six days. The seventh day was then set aside by God as a day of rest. The "days of man" are six, during which he labors to provide his daily bread. It is interesting that the number 6 is the number of man in the Scriptures, and 666, the mark of the beast, is the glorification of the man who aspires to take the place of God.

One day is for the Lord. Scripture states in several places that one day in God's sight is as a thousand years. The beginning of time, according to Usher's chronology, took place at 4004 B.C. Now it is true that there were mistakes in his calculations, and problems down through the centuries with the keeping of an exact record of the years. The theory of the "Day of the Lord" changes one day into a thousand years, a millennium, making six thousand years for man, and one thousand for God, the time that the Bible calls the Millennium. If the world was created at somewhere around B.C. 4000, then the six thousand years for man would be over around 2000 A.D. And the Rapture of the church followed by the Great Tribulation, and then the millennial reign of Christ is soon to begin. The problem, of course, is that the original date of 4004 B.C. is quite inaccurate, plus the fact that the Bible does not directly teach this, so we can only take it as an interesting theory. Christ may come at any time.

The "Canopied Earth" theory

Another theory about the earth we live in is called the theory of the canopied and recanopied earth. Many of God's scholars, such as Professor Howard Kellogg and C. Theo Schwartze, hold to the belief that when God made the heavens and the earth, He enclosed the earth in a canopy of water turned to ice. Astronomers tell us that five of the eight planets in our solar system have canopies around them. If the earth also had a canopy, one made of water or ice instead of gasses, this would account for the absence of rain before the Flood. The earth was watered by a mist that went up from the ground. It would also account for the long life of people during those first hundreds of years after creation, as the dangerous ultraviolet rays of the sun would not get through to the earth. It possibly could account for Noah's drunkenness after drinking wine when he left the ark. There would have been no fermentation during that first period of earth's history, therefore Noah would not have known that he would get drunk. At the Flood God melted the canopy and left the earth exposed to the sun's rays. Life quickly shortened and degeneration set in. In the book of Revelation, chapter 21, verse 1, we read that after God creates new heavens and a new earth, there will be no more sea. Why? What will happen to the sea? The earth will be destroyed by fire turning the water to vapor that will rise. High up this will turn to ice, forming a canopy around the earth again, and making ideal Edenic conditions on the earth. Symbolically, sea speaks of separation, of which there will be none in God's perfect world. Now this is another interesting theory, and quite probably true. Yet we do not have enough Scripture to assert definitely that this is the way it was and this is the way it will be. One day all will be clarified.

PART 2

THE PRESENTATION OF THE NEW JERUSALEM

Before we get into the presentation and description of the New Jerusalem, the words of Dr. L.E. Maxwell, founder and first president of Prairie Bible Institute, and my professor of the book of Revelation, come to my mind. Before he launched into the study of the book of Revelation, he first asked us members of the class to make him a promise. He asked us to promise that when all of the prophecies of the book have been fulfilled, and we share the glories of the heavenly home, that we will not go to him and say: "Dr. Maxwell, do you remember how you taught the book of Revelation back there at Prairie?" True, while there are many things we can know and be sure of, or we would never have been given the book, yet interpretations do abound, and we should not be too dogmatic about our particular way of looking at the events and descriptions of the end times. You may disagree with my interpretations, and this is your privilege. If you prefer being wrong, that's your right. Just kidding. It may seem to you that I am being too dogmatic at times, but please remember that I am simply presenting things the way I see them. I must do this to be honest and true to my own convictions. And with these words I launch out.

Chapter Five
A Panoramic View Of The New Jerusalem

It is an eternal city.

Not many things are eternal. Wherever we look there is change. People change. You are not the same person this year as you were last. Countries change. Take a look at a modern map of the world, and marvel at the changes that have taken place in this world since you were in school. Deterioration, decay and destruction face us every day of our lives. Food spoils; metal rusts; clothes get moth eaten; wood rots; flowers wilt. Go back to your home town, to your home church, to the place where you were born, and note the many changes that have taken place.

But some things really are eternal. God's Word is eternal. It is unchanging. People are eternal. God gave us eternal souls, so that after the death of this body in which we temporarily reside, there will be a resurrection. Of course, God is the one eternal and never changing Being behind His Word and the people that He has created. And He has an eternal home for those that have been redeemed through the blood of His Son, the Lord Jesus Christ. This eternal city is called the New Jerusalem.

Let's take a look at *1 Peter 1:3-4*.

"Blessed be the God and Father of our Lord Jesus Christ, who according to His great mercy has caused us to be born again to a living hope through the resurrection of Jesus Christ from

the dead, to obtain an inheritance which is imperishable and undefiled and will not fade away, reserved in heaven for you." (NAS)

Those of us who have been born again have a living hope. A blessed hope! A glorious inheritance awaits us. Since it is imperishable, no agent of deterioration can produce any change whatsoever in it. It reminds me of the words of the Lord Jesus concerning matters of the heart. He counseled his disciples as follows:

"Do not lay up for yourselves treasures upon earth, where moth and rust destroy, and where thieves break in and steal. But lay up for yourselves treasures in heaven, where neither moth nor rust destroys, and where thieves do not break in or steal." (Matthew 6:19-20 NAS)

This inheritance is not and will never be defiled by any source of contamination. No smog will fill the air, as in most of the cities of today. The River of Life will contain no pollution of any kind. And this glorious inheritance of ours will not fade away. Unlike the glory that shone on the face of Moses when he came down from the presence of God on Mount Sinai. Unlike colorful curtains that have been too long in bright sunlight. Unlike the mist of the morning. Our blessed inheritance will not change at all. God's city is eternal. Unchanging.

It is a literal city.

Is the New Jerusalem a literal city or just symbolic of the church? Is it a real, actual city or just a figurative, symbolic city? Though it has much symbolism in its description, I believe that it is a real, literal city. Why? Let me give you some reasons why I believe that it is a literal city.

REASONS WHY THE NEW JERUSALEM IS A LITERAL CITY

1. The Old Testament saints looked for a literal city of God, a heavenly city built by God. Take a look at the following verses from Hebrews chapter 11, from the great Hall of Fame of God's heroes.

About Abraham we read:

"For he was looking for the city which has foundations, whose architect and builder is God." (Verse 10 NAS)

Referring to Abel, Enoch, Noah, Abraham, and Sarah, the writer concludes:

"All these died in faith, without receiving the promises, but having seen them and having welcomed them from a distance, and having confessed that they were strangers and exiles on the earth. For those who say such things make it clear that they are seeking a country of their own. And indeed if they had been thinking of that country from which they went out, they would have had opportunity to return. But as it is, they desire a better country, that is a heavenly one. Therefore God is not ashamed to be called their God, for He has prepared a city for them." (Verses 13-16 NAS)

Chapters 12 and 13 of Hebrews adds two more verses about the awaited city.

"But you have come to Mount Zion and to the city of the living God, the heavenly Jerusalem, and to myriads of angels." (12:22 NAS)

"For here we do not have a lasting city, but we are seeking the city which is to come." (13:14 NAS)

The Millennial Jerusalem could not be this city because it does not fit the description of the millennial city as given in given in Ezekiel 40. That city did not come down from heaven. It will be built in Israel. It is not heavenly but earthly, not made by God but by man. It will have a temple there with sacrifices reinstituted. The New Jerusalem has no temple and no sacrifices.

2. The fact that the angel called John to come and see the bride, but what he actually saw was the New Jerusalem, does not necessarily mean that the New Jerusalem is the bride. It could mean that the bride is in the New Jerusalem. Thus **Revelation 21:9-10** would mean that the bride is in the city, not that it is the city. We'll get into this in more detail later.

3. The description of the New Jerusalem includes details that could not be applied to the church. For instance, **Revelation 21:24-27** states that the kings of the earth will bring their glory into it. How could they bring their glory into the church? They will bring their glory to God. There will be no night there. The word "there" indicates a place. The city is a place. Those whose names are in the Book of Life will enter it. But if the city is the church, they are already in it. If they are not, how can they enter a symbolic city?

4. The many details in the description of the New Jerusalem (walls, gates, street, light, foundations, etc.) make it difficult to believe that this is all figurative language and that no such place exists. A Bible teacher often would tell the class that when the passage in question makes sense as it is, there is no need to look for any other meaning. True.

5. The chief objection to this being a literal city appears to be the difficulty in conceiving of a city shaped like a cube. How could there be a throne, a river, a street, and trees in a cube? However, if it is not a cube but a mountain, this objection disappears.

6. When John was told to come and see the bride of Christ, he looked and said he saw a city, the New Jerusalem. Would he have said that if looking at a cube? Probably not. What John saw evidently looked enough like a city for him to call it a city and enough like the old Jerusalem that he had seen many times for him to call it the New Jerusalem.

7. The city is said to be a square, **Revelation 21:16**, never a cube. It is on the new and heavenly Mt. Zion, **Hebrews 12:22**. Some of the description of the Mountain of the House of the Lord in Isaiah 2 could only apply to this New Jerusalem, such as no more war. There will be war at the end of the millennium.

For the above reasons it seems logical to me that the figurative language used throughout chapters 21 and 22 of the book of Revelation do not require that the whole city be taken as figurative and symbolical. Though much of the description has symbolism in it, the city itself is a literal city.

It is a holy city.

The cities of today are hotbeds of crime, drugs, vices of all kinds, and poverty. Not so the New Jerusalem. **Revelation 21:2** is John's testimony of what he saw.

"And I saw the holy city, new Jerusalem, coming down out of heaven from God, prepared as a bride adorned for her husband." (RSV)

John calls it a holy city. No lies will ever be told there; no shady business deals will be transacted; no scams will be perpetrated on innocent people; no filthy words or swearing will be heard; no arguing or fighting will take place; no one will steal from another; there will be no pornography, sleazy magazines, or unwholesome literature of any kind. In fact, no sin of any kind. There will not be any police, lawyers, judges, or jails in that city. It will be a city of unlocked doors, symbolically speaking. The city will be holy because all of its citizens will be holy.

It is a beautiful city.

"And I, John, saw the Holy City, the new Jerusalem, coming down from God out of heaven. It was a glorious sight, beautiful as a bride at her wedding." (Revelation 21:2 LB)

" Then one of the seven angels, who had emptied the flasks containing the seven last plagues, came and said to me: 'Come with me and I will show you the bride the Lamb's wife.' In a vision he took me to a towering mountain peak and from there I watched that wondrous city, the holy Jerusalem, descending out of the skies from God. It was filled with the glory of God, and flashed and glowed like a precious gem, crystal clear like jasper." (Revelation 21:9-11 LB)

What a magnificent sight! This great city had the beauty of a bride adorned for her husband at the wedding. Few will dispute the fact that a woman is never more beautiful than at her wedding. It is not only because of her beautiful dress and ornaments, but due also to the inner glow that radiates in her facial expression. I remember when I stood at the altar many years ago and watched my wife-to-be coming down the aisle. Wow! Could anyone be more lovely? It stands to reason that this city would be compared to a bride, since it is the eternal home of the bride of Christ. Back in ***Revelation 19:7*** we read:

"Let us rejoice and be glad and give Him glory! For the wedding of the Lamb has come, and his bride has made herself ready." (NIV)

John was amazed as he watched that glorious city descending from heaven. It was filled with the glory of God, and shone like a precious jewel. Wycliffe Bible Commentary makes this statement: "All the beautiful things in the world that God has made: sunsets, mountains, lakes, roses, beautiful trees, snowflakes, clouds, waterfalls. What will a city be like made by the divine architect?"

There will be no smog to cloud the sky and dim the vision, no dirty streets and unkempt yards, no ugly unpainted buildings, no trash heaps or garbage disposals, no slums for the poor. All will be beauty and glory far beyond anything we have ever seen or can even imagine. The apostle Paul made this ecstatic statement:

"For I consider that the sufferings of this present time are not worthy to be compared with the glory that is to be revealed to us." (Romans 8:18 NAS)

Cities are both buildings and people. We may say: "Seattle is a very pretty city," and be talking about the buildings, streets, parks, riverfront, etc. Or we could say: "Seattle is a wicked city, a bustling city, a friendly city," and, of course, we would be referring to the people. It appears that John is seeing the people more than the buildings in this global vision of ***Revelation 21:1-4***.

Who is this bride? She is the bride of Christ, His church. Let's look at a few verses about the bride.

"Therefore, my brethren, you also have become dead to the law through the body of Christ, that you may be married to another - to Him who was raised from the dead, that we should bear fruit to God." (Romans 7:4 NKJ)

"Husbands, love your wives, just as Christ also loved the church and gave Himself up for her; that He might sanctify her, having cleansed her by the washing of water with the word, that He might present to Himself the church in all her glory, having no spot or wrinkle or any such thing; but that she should be holy and blameless." (Ephesians 5:25-27 NAS)

"For I am jealous for you with a godly jealousy; for I betrothed you to one husband, that to Christ I might present you as a pure virgen." (2 Corinthians 11:2 NAS)

We have previously asked the question: Is the church the city or is the church in the city? In other words, are we to take the New Jerusalem as a literal city or a symbolic city, representing the church. We have already seen that it is a literal city. But like the tabernacle, it is full of symbolism. It is not the church, but is the eternal home of the church, an incredibly beautiful place that Christ prepared for us, according to ***John 14:2***.

"In My Father's house are many dwelling places. if it were not so, I would have told you, for I go to prepare a place for you." (NAS)

Can you imagine a place that has been in the making for 2,000 years, with Christ Himself as the architect and builder? This is our eternal home. What a glorious hope we have set before us!

The following illustration is highly inadequate to describe the beautiful picture before us, but it does show in a small way what a change it will be for those of us who know Christ as our Savior. There is a little town in Venezuela called Sanare, where my wife and I would go occasionally for a short rest. It is nestled up in the mountains, only a couple of hours drive from where we lived in the city of Barquisimeto. The highway goes through barren land until you begin to climb. Then suddenly you burst out between the hills and a beautiful panoramic view stretches out ahead of you. The fields are a lush green, with farms here and there, lakes scattered all over, and mountains on the other side. What a difference from the dry, arid, almost wasteland, that we went through to get there. It seemed like heaven to us. But, of course, what God has prepared for us will far exceed anything that we may ever enjoy here on earth.

It is interesting to make a comparison between man's first home and his last, the Garden of Eden in Gen. 1-2 and the New Jerusalem in Revelation 20-21, the first two and the last two chapters of the Bible. The similarities are striking.

A COMPARISON OF GENESIS 1-2 AND REVELATION 21-22

GENESIS 1-2	REVELATION 21-22
1. The Garden of Eden	The New Jerusalem
2. Man's first home	Man's last home.
3. Creation (1:1)	Re-creation (21:1)
4. Canopied earth (?) (1:6-8)	Recanopied earth (?)
5. Light without sun (1:1-5)	Light without sun (21:23)
6. Man in the image of God (1:26)	The saved bear the likeness of Christ (1 John 3:2)
7. Man is perfect, without sin. (Romans 5:12)	The saved are perfected forever. (21:1 and 27 and Hebrews 10:14)

8. First Adam rules creation. (1:28)	Last Adam (Christ) rules all creation (22:3, Isaiah 9:6-7)
9. No sickness or death (Rom. 5:12)	No sickness, trials, or death (21:4)
10. Man given work to do (2:15)	The saved serve the Lord. (22:3)
11. Man's diet is vegetarian. (1:29)	Man eats fruit from the Tree Of Life (22:2)
12. Man gets a bride. (2:18-24)	Christ gets a bride. (21:2 and 9)
13. A river flows from Eden to water the garden. (2:10)	The River of Life flows from the throne to water the land. (22:1-2)
14. God is present in the garden. (3:8)	God dwells among men. (21:3)
15. The ground is not yet cursed. (3:17)	The curse is removed. (22:3)
16. The Tree of Life is located there. (2:9)	The Tree of Life lines both sides of the River of Life. (22:2)
17. There is no tabernacle, temple or church in the Garden.	No temple there. (21:22)
18. The Garden of Eden is Paradise.	The New Jerusalem is Paradise restored. (Revelation 2:7)
19. The Garden of Eden was planted by God. (Gen. 2:8)	The New Jerusalem was built by God. (Hebrews 11:10 with Revelation 21:2)

Yes, man's last home will be very similar to his first home in the Garden of Eden. It will be an absolutely beautiful place, this city of God, where the ransomed of the earth will enjoy the presence and fellowship of God throughout eternity. Hallelujah!

God Himself will be there.

"I heard a loud voice from the throne saying, "Look, the home of God is now among men, and he will live with them and they will be his people; yes, God himself will be among them." (Revelation 21:3 LB)

The word translated "home" in this version is "tabernacle" in some other versions of the Bible. God will tabernacle among us. In other words God will pitch his tent among men. Emmanuel, God with us, will literally come true. In **John 1:14** John declares:

"And the Word became flesh and dwelt among us, and we beheld His glory..."(NAS)

A Panoramic View Of The New Jerusalem

Those who knew Jesus in that day saw His glory, just a fleeting glimpse of a little of His glory. Then we will see Him face to face, not just for a few years but forever. All of his glory will dazzle our eyes. We will not only see it, but will share in it as well. The hymn writer had this in mind, when he penned the well known lines:

When all my labors and trials are o'er,
And I am safe on that beautiful shore,
Just to be near the dear Lord I adore,
Will through the ages be glory for me.

O that will be glory for me, glory for me, glory for me.
When by his grace I shall look on his face.
That will be glory, be glory for me.

When by the gift of his infinite grace,
I am accorded in heaven a place,
Just to be there and to look on his face
Will through the ages be glory for me.

Friends will be there I have loved long ago;
Joy like a river around me will flow;
Yet just a smile from my Savior I know,
Will through the ages be glory for me.

Charles H. Gabriel

The last chapters of the book of Ezekiel describe in detail the glories of the millennial Jerusalem and especially the temple. The millennium will be a glorious time of peace and prosperity. I especially like the last verse of the book, where Ezekiel, under the inspiration of the Holy Spirit, puts the capstone on the blessedness of this millennial period with these words:

> *"...and the name of the city from that day shall be, 'The Lord is there.'" (Ezekiel 48:35 NAS)*

If this is true of the millennium, how much more of the New Jerusalem. God Himself will be present. What an awesome thought!

All trials and tragedies will be over.

> *"He will wipe away all tears from their eyes, and there shall be no more death, nor sorrow, nor crying, nor pain. All of that has gone forever." (Revelation 21:4 LB)*

What tears are these that God will wipe away? Perhaps tears shed at the Judgment Seat of Christ. Perhaps tears that are left over from all the trials and heartaches of life here on earth. For the ladies, perhaps tears of joy. Oops! Not only the ladies, but all of us may be shedding tears of joy in that day.

Will there be sexual distinctions in that heavenly home? Christ did say that there will not be marriage, for we will all be like the angels of God. However, this probably does not mean that there will not be sexual distinctions, since we get there through the resurrection, and not through a new and different creation. These same old bodies will be resurrected and transformed.

At any rate we know that no one there will ever cry again from pain, sorrow, or death. All semblance of trials and tragedies are gone forever. Our newly resurrected and transformed bodies will not be able to experience pain. No one will ever get sick, or cough and sneeze from allergies, or need surgery to correct some physical problem. None will ever go through radiation or chemotherapy due to the ravages of cancer.

There will be no doctors, nurses, hospitals or clinics. Since death will be abolished, for only life results from God's presence, there will be no mourning the dead, no caskets, graves, cemeteries, funeral processions, or morticians. The old life with all of its heartaches and trials will be forever past, and new life in Christ will take its place. Amen! What a glorious day that will be!

All of the trials and tribulations that we presently experience are a direct consequence of the Fall, of the sin of Adam and Eve in disobeying God by eating of the fruit that He had forbidden. Sin entered into the world at that time with all of its ramifications and results. Man's nature became sinful. The wickedness of man has led to drug addiction, slavery, prostitution, thievery, murder, and the whole gamut of human suffering. Sickness became an integral part of the human story. God even put a curse upon the earth. Read about it in ***Genesis 3:17-19:***

"Cursed is the ground because of you; In toil you shall eat of it all the days of your life. Both thorns and thistles it shall grow for you; and you shall eat the plants of the field; By the sweat of your face you shall eat bread, till you return to the ground, because from it you were taken; for you are dust, and to dust you shall return." (NAS)

Anyone who has ever done any gardening knows how true these statements are. Thorns and thistles. Weeds. How easily they grow! Have you ever seen a package of weed seeds? No need for it. Weeds require no seeding, no cultivation of the soil, no watering. They grow automatically. But try to get a good harvest of vegetables, and that's another story. It takes cultivation, planting carefully according to the instructions of the seed packet, weeding, watering, etc. Toil! I must say that I do enjoy it, but that's because it is a hobby for me. I love to see things grow. One year I planted New Zealand spinach, according to the packet of seeds, but when it came up, it didn't really look like spinach. Oh well, it supposedly was New Zealand spinach, a different variety. We began to cut off the plants and eat them in salads. As the plants grew taller, they looked less and less like normal spinach. They began to produce heads on them. Heads? On spinach? Turned out that it was really broccoli. How broccoli seeds got into the spinach packet I'll never know. Actually they didn't taste bad raw. Perhaps a little bitter, but very edible. I must confess that we felt a little embarrassed with the friends to whom we had given our "New Zealand spinach". I didn't have the heart to tell at least one friend that we had given her broccoli. With others that we were on more familiar terms with we just had a good laugh.

I don't share the opinion of some who seem to feel that God's statement that man would eat the plants of the field is a part of the curse. "Broccoli, cauliflower, spinach, squash, ugh!" they say. However, I take the curse to be limited to the laborious work with little productivity that is involved in making a living. Farmers work hard, from early in the morning until sunset or later. In the New Jerusalem there will be no more curse on the ground. ***Revelation 22:3*** states simply:

"And there shall no longer be any curse..." (NAS)

The curse will be lifted when the old world is destroyed by fire and God makes a new one. The ground that grows the tree of life will not be under the curse. It is quite possible that the works of service that God's redeemed will be engaged in will include tending this beautiful garden, just as Adam and Eve in the perfect environment of the new creation were told to cultivate and keep the Garden of Eden. If so, we can look forward to pleasant activity in another perfect environment. Yes, all toil, trials, and tribulations will be ended for God's people.

I had the privilege of serving the Lord with the Orinoco River Mission in Venezuela for a number of years, and during the first five years I was involved in launch evangelism on the Orinoco River, along with several others. The Orinoco is a mighty river, swift and turbulent during the dry season and wide and deep during the rainy season. There is a difference of some fifty to seventy feet between the low point during the dry season and the high point during the rainy season. Navigation at times is difficult and even dangerous. Sandbars and rocks come to the surface during the dry season. Storms can come up suddenly.

On one occasion we were headed back to our home port of Ciudad Bolivar at the close of a trip. The trip had been uneventful until we got closer to Ciudad Bolivar. Suddenly we noticed that the water up ahead had turned blackish in color. This usually meant a storm was coming and the wind was pushing the waves upriver. We were anxious to get back home, and decided to continue. It didn't look that bad. At least not until it hit us. Then it was too late to head for shore. I was piloting the launch at the time and did my best to hit every wave head on and at a reduced speed. A Venezuelan fellow, who worked with us at the time, climbed all over the launch and tied down anything that might get blown away. As it was, we lost the gangplank overboard, and a cabinet top deck came crashing down. A missionary lady on board went down below deck and gave up her dinner. Not too happily, I'm sure. Ugh! Seasickness is no fun. We continued to hit all the waves head on, because if we would have gotten turned sideways to a wave and fallen into the trough that opened up, we probably would have capsized. The boat is nearly flat bottomed so as to be able to dock in shallow ports. When it grew dark, we shone our spotlight on the waves and could see the crests. Gradually we drew near to an island. When we got into the shelter of the island, though the waves were still quite high, we were able to spin the launch around by putting one engine in forward and the other in reverse. Now heading upriver against the current, the launch slowed down rapidly, and we found a place to dock and spend the night. Our first activity was to gather together and have a time of prayer and praise to God for bringing us through. Someday we will tie up our ship on that golden shore, and all the storms and trials of life will be forever past. What a glorious hope is ours!

PART 3

THE DESCRIPTION OF THE NEW JERUSALEM

The sweet singer of Israel, David, closed his beautiful Psalm 23 with these words: "And I will dwell in the house of the Lord forever." Abraham, the great father of faith, looked for a city, "whose builder and maker is God." Christ promised His disciples that He would prepare a place for them. All three, David, Abraham, and Jesus, were talking about the same place. The house of the Lord is the city of God, the New Jerusalem, that Christ went to prepare for His people to be their eternal dwelling place.

Chapter Six
A Closer Look

Its Glory

There follows in Revelation 21 a description of this great and holy city, the New Jerusalem. John was carried away to a high mountain to get a good view of the New Jerusalem as it descended from heaven to the earth. He saw the city in all its glory, but focused on its people, the bride of Christ in the first four verses of this chapter. Then in the following verses he focuses on the city itself and gives us a description of its walls, gates, gatekeepers, foundation stones, size, materials, street, river, light, and food. The city glows like a crystal clear jasper stone, since its foundation is a jasper stone, and the city itself is made of pure transparent gold. It glows with the glory of God. It is like the Shekinah glory of God in the Old Testament, as set forth in the following verses:

"And it came about as Aaron spoke to the whole congregation of the sons of Israel, that they looked toward the wilderness, and behold, the glory of the Lord appeared in the cloud." (Exodus 16:10 NAS)

"Then Moses went up to the mountain, and the cloud covered the mountain. And the glory of the Lord rested on Mount Sinai, and the cloud covered it for six days; and on the seventh day he called to Moses from the midst of the cloud. And to the eyes of the sons of Israel the appearance of the glory of the Lord was like a

consuming fire on the mountain top." (Exodus 24:15-17 NAS)

"Then the glory of the Lord appeared in the tent of meeting to all the sons of Israel." (Numbers 14:10b NAS)

"And when the priests came forth from the holy place...and all the Levitical singers..., clothed in fine linen...and with them one hundred and twenty priests blowing trumpets in unison with the trumpeters and the singers were to make themselves heard with one voice to praise and to glorify the Lord..., then the house, the house of the Lord, was filled with a cloud so that the priests could not stand to minister because of the cloud, for the glory of the Lord filled the house of God." (2 Chronicles 5:11-14 NAS)

Its Size and Shape

Let's listen to the words of the apostle John as he tells about this unusual and magnificent city.

"The one talking with me had a golden measuring rod to measure the city with its gates and its walls. The city is laid out as a quadrangle, with its length equal to its width. With the rod he measured the city, about fifteen hundred miles—the length, the width and the height exactly equal." (Revelation 21:15-16 ML)

The 12,000 stadia that other translations ascribe to the length, width and height of the city amounts to about 1500 miles. Can you imagine a city of this size? Fifteen hundred miles! That would cover about half of the continental United States. One city! Then the question is - how is it shaped? Is it a cube, a pyramid or

A Closer Look

a cone? John states that it is a square with the length and width both about 1500 miles. He never states that it is a cube, as many Bible interpreters picture it. If this city were an actual cube, since its height is also 1500 miles, it would be like something that we have never seen, and find it difficult to imagine. Of course, God could make it a cube with compartments or apartments all through it, as clear as crystal so the light could shine through it. But where would the river flow, and where would the throne of God be located? All of this is very difficult to imagine and we would need to take it by faith alone. However, I do not believe that the New Jerusalem is shaped like a cube. It could also be a pyramid or a cone, and still have the same height. Or it could it be a mountain? There are a number of Scripture verses in the book of Isaiah that talk about the "mountain of the house of the Lord." *(Isaiah 2:1-4, 27:13, 66:20)* During the Millennium God's house will be located on Mt. Zion. But where will the New Jerusalem after the Millennium be located? In *Hebrews 12:22* the writer gives this information:

"But you have come to Mount Zion, to the heavenly Jerusalem, the city of the living God." (NIV)

Whoa! The heavenly Jerusalem is located on Mt. Zion! This could not be the earthly Mt. Zion as it would be far too small to hold it. Could it be another mountain, also called Mt. Zion as indicative of God's presence? How else can we interpret that verse? I picture the New Jerusalem as a mountain as high as it is long and wide, with the throne of God at the summit and the River of Life flowing out from the throne and around the mountain as it descends to the bottom and flows out into the renewed earth. It flows in the middle of the wide street that encircles the mountain, perhaps a hundred thousand miles long, with mansions or dwelling places on both sides of it. Just supposing the highway and river measure one mile down to the next lap, you would encircle the mountain 1500 times getting to the bottom, that last circuit being about 6,000 miles long. Amazing! Yet believable. Remember it is the home of all the redeemed of all ages, so a lot of room will be needed to provide the dwelling places for all. Of course, we have no idea what these will look like, or with our resurrected bodies if we will have need of a house such as we now use. All I ask is that when we get there, you don't come around to me and say: "Harold, do you remember how you described the New Jerusalem back when we were in our earthly bodies?"

At the close of this chapter is a drawing of what I conceive to be the shape of this glorious city, along with illustrations of the foundation and wall of the city, and its street with the river of life running through the middle of it and the tree of life on both sides of the river.

Its Walls and Gates

John's description of the great city continues:

"It had a great and high wall, with twelve gates, and at the gates twelve angels, and names were written on them, which are those of the twelve tribes of the sons of Israel. There were three gates on the east and three gates on the north and three gates on the south and three gates on the west. And the wall of the city had twelve foundation stones, and on them were the twelve names of the twelve apostles of the Lamb."

A Closer Look

"And he measured its wall, seventy two yards according to human measurements, which are also angelic measurements. And the material of the wall was jasper; and the city was pure gold, like clear glass. The foundation stones of the city wall were adorned with every kind of precious stone. The first foundation stone was jasper, the second, sapphire; the third, chalcedony; the fourth, emerald; the fifth, sardonyx; the sixth, sardius; the seventh, chrysolite; the eighth, beryl; the ninth, topaz; the tenth, chrysoprase; the eleventh, jacinth; the twelfth, amethyst. And the twelve gates were twelve pearls; each one of the gates was a single pearl." (Revelation 21:12-14, 17-21a NAS)

One wonders why such a great and beautiful city in a world without Satan and sin would need a wall around it. There was no need for it. But God evidently wanted it to be clearly recognizable as a city of those days. Jerusalem was a walled city. Other cities had walls. This was what the people were accustomed to seeing. Their walls were for protection against the enemies around them. Not this wall. Yet the Lord uses things we are familiar with to show us things He wants to teach or show us. This is another reason why I doubt that the city is a cube in shape. It would be unrecognizable as a city.

And what a wall! Seventy two yards, or 216 feet high, about the height of a 24 story building! There were twelve gates in the wall, three on each side, with angelic gatekeepers. The Living Bible adds the thought that the twelve gates were guarded by the twelve angels. This is an interpretation not in the text. I prefer thinking that these twelve angels were receptionists, not guards, there to welcome those who would enter the gates. The names of the twelve tribes of Israel were written on the gates. Each gate was made of a single pearl. Wow! What a pearl! Unbelievable in size and beauty! But why were the gates made of pearl? Perhaps the following two verses tell us the reason.

"I am the door, if anyone enters through Me, he shall be saved, and shall go in and out, and find pasture." (John 10:9 NAS)

"Again, the kingdom of heaven is like a merchant seeking fine pearls, and upon finding one pearl of great value, he went and sold all that he had, and bought it." (Matthew 13:45-46 NAS)

The subject of both of these parables is the Lord Jesus Christ. He is the door to heaven, and there is no other way. No other gate. He is the pearl of great price that makes one willing to give up all else to obtain. And so the New Jerusalem has gates made of pearl. Christ, the pearl of great price, is the gate into that beautiful city.

The beautiful lines of a hymn I love explains this a little more.

He the pearly gates will open,
So that I may enter in.
For He purchased my redemption,
And forgave me all my sin."

Frederick A. Blohm

The material of the wall around the city is pure jasper with twelve foundation stones of precious jewels. Again the living Bible adds a new dimension to this picture by translating it as twelve layers of precious stones, one on top of the other. Since most

people are unfamiliar with the types of stones that are listed here, quite different than the stones builders use in today's foundations, I will list them with their colors.
1. Jasper - opaque green
2. Sapphire - opaque blue
3. Chalcedony - emerald of greenish hue
4. Emerald - transparent green
5. Sardonyx - red and white
6. Sardius - bright red
7. Chrysolite - bright yellow
8. Beryl - bluish green
9. Topaz - greenish yellow
10. Chrysoprase - a darker shade of yellowish green
11. Jacinth - sky blue
12. Amethyst - violet

Can you imagine for a moment the beauty of that foundation? The wall of jasper covered with stones of such different and brilliant colors will form a stunning multicolored mosaic. The harmony and breathtaking beauty of the colors have been compared with the rainbow.

Another question that may come to your mind about the names on the gates and on the foundation is why wasn't it reversed. One would expect the gates to be named after the apostles and the foundation after the tribes of the sons of Israel, since foundations are laid before the gates are put in. Again let us look to the Scriptures to see if we can locate a reason for this. Jesus stated to the Samaritan woman in *John 4:22* that:

"*...salvation is from the Jews.*" *(NAS)*

The entrance to salvation came through the Jewish people, Jesus Christ Himself being a Jew. He is the door to the sheepfold, the gate to heaven and the New Jerusalem, yet He is the "root and the offspring of David," *(Revelation 22:16)* We owe much to the Jew,

God's chosen race, so it is appropriate that the gates to this eternal city have Jewish names on them. I read somewhere that this layout of the city surrounded by the wall with gates bearing the names of the 12 tribes of Israel is a picture of the tabernacle surrounded by the 12 tribes of Israel as they traveled toward the promised land as set forth in the book of Numbers.

As to the foundations of the city being named after the apostles, we can turn to *Ephesians 2:20-21* for verification as to why they were so named.

"Having been built upon the foundation of the apostles and prophets, Christ Jesus Himself being the corner stone, in whom the whole building being fitted together is growing into a holy temple in the Lord." (NAS)

The apostles, along with the New Testament prophets, laid the foundation of the church through their ministry and the Scripture that they wrote. And so the eternal home of the church will have the names of the 12 apostles on its foundation.

Its Street and River

"And the street of the city was made of pure gold, as transparent as glass." (Revelation 21:21b ML)

"And He pointed out to me a river of pure Water of Life, clear as crystal, flowing from the throne of God and the Lamb, coursing down the center of the main street. On each side of the river grew Trees of Life, bearing twelve crops of fruit, with a fresh crop each month; the leaves were used for medicine to heal the nations." (Revelation 22:1-2 LB)

A Closer Look

You would expect that a city the size of half of the United States would have streets, highways, freeways, and roads criss-crossing it in all directions. Not so this glorious city. Twice the word "street" is used, and both times it is in the singular. There will be only one street in the New Jerusalem. Only one street? Is there some symbolism hidden behind this? Christ stated in **John 14:6:**

"I am the way...no one comes to the Father but through me." (NAS)

He is the one way, the only way into the presence of God, the only way to the New Jerusalem. All who travel there must take this way, this street. And so even in this city, so full of symbolism, there is only one street, symbolic of the uniqueness of Christ as the only way.

The Greek word for street suggests a wide avenue or boulevard. It is paved with pure gold, as transparent as glass. Flawless! Gold is the metal of royalty. Christ is King of Kings and Lord of Lords. Transparency speaks of perfection. This is the real King's Highway with no potholes or ruts, no bumps or rocks, the smoothest surface that you could possibly imagine. This street is a divided avenue. There is a river flowing down the center of the street, the River of Life. The River of Life! Like the water of life, or living water, that Christ offered to the Samaritan woman! Let's look at some Scripture verses that speak of this life.

"Jesus said to him, 'I am the...life." (John 14:6 NAS)

"I came that they might have life, and might have it abundantly" (John 10:10b NAS)

"...but whoever drinks of the water that I shall give him shall never thirst; but the water that I shall give him shall become in him a well

***of water springing up to eternal life." (John 4:14 NAS*)**

It is interesting to note that the word in Greek for "drink" in ***John 4:14*** is in the aorist tense, which gives a point of time. One event. This is the drink of salvation, pointing to that blessed day when you received Christ as your Savior and drank of the Water of Life. Look back at the previous verse in this chapter, and again one finds the word "drink." Jesus explains to the Samaritan woman that everyone who drinks of the water of the well shall thirst again. Here the word "drink" is in the present tense in Greek. This speaks of continued or repeated action. One must drink often because thirst keeps coming back. This can be applied not only to physical natural water, but to all the world offers as well. One is never fully satisfied and must keep coming back for more. Yet one drink of the Water that Christ offers, the salvation drink, provides a well of water that springs up to life eternal.

What a joy it is to actually watch while a thirsty soul deeply drinks of that water of life for the first time! Let me tell you about Ana. It all happened one sunny day, while my three sons were home from high school. We were living in the city of San Felipe in Venezuela and starting a church there. The house we lived in was huge with four bedrooms, three bathrooms, living room, family room, dining room, utility room, and kitchen. A perfect place to start a church. We soon had Sunday School classes meeting in the utility room, which became my office, in a bedroom, the living room, the family room, and even the kitchen. Below the house was a large basement that we could drive our car into at night, which became the meeting place for the church after the large living room filled up.

In front of the house a wide cement walkway, covered with a flowering vine, led to the street. That vine had grown so much that it was weighing down the lead pipes on which it grew. One Sunday morning a snake fell down from the vine, and scared the children half to death. They screamed. Several men immediately dashed up from the meeting in the basement and killed the snake. It was time to trim the vine. So that sunny day my boys and I decided to get out the machete and cut the vine. I was busy lopping off long branches of the vine which my boys hauled off to a vacant lot, when suddenly a well-dressed lady came down the street and stopped at our house. She asked for the pastor of the church. Probably thought that I was the gardener. I looked the part with my dirty clothes and machete in my hand. I abashedly presented myself as the pastor. She had come for counsel, but this was apparently not the time, so we arranged a later date during that week. When Ana came back, I was better dressed and better prepared to receive her. In my office she poured out her sad story, one often heard there, of a husband who was losing contact with her and their three children. Ana wept as she recounted the events that led her to come to see me. Her husband had another woman, and spent time and money on her that he should have given to his family. Years of married life, three children, a seemingly happy family, everything she held dear, seemed to be going down the drain. I was glad that I could tell her about One who is always faithful and will never leave us, One who loved us so much that He gave His life on the Cross to be able to receive us into His family. After I explained all this to Ana, I asked her if she would like to receive Christ as her Savior. Without hesitation she replied that she would. We prayed. Ana asked Jesus to come into her life and help her. I prayed for her and her situation. I have never in all my years of ministry in Venezuela or in the States seen someone change as radically as Ana changed that day. She entered the house with a heavy load, and cried as she related the cause. Now the load of care had been lifted, and she left with a smile on her face. She had taken that first drink of the water of life. I wish we could tell you that her husband then changed his ways and returned to the family, but such is not the case. He did leave them, but Ana has remained faithful to the Lord, her constant companion.

The River of Life flows through the middle of the King's Highway, giving life to all that it reaches. It is only as Christ and His teachings permeate every area of our life that we will enjoy life more abundantly. All that is cut off from that life tends to die. We must "abide in Him" to maintain that abundant life that comes from constant fellowship with the fountain of life, Christ Himself.

Where is the source of the River of Life? It comes out of the throne of God and the Lamb. If the New Jerusalem is a mountain, as I believe it is, the everlasting mountain of the house of the Lord, with God's throne situated on the summit at the peak of the mountain, the River of Life flows forth from under the throne and begins its descent of the mountain. God is the source of all good things, of all life. James, the half-brother of Jesus, states in his book, chapter one and verse 17 these words:

"Every good thing bestowed and every perfect gift is from above, coming down from the Father of lights, with whom there is no variation, or shifting shadow." (NAS)

Now let's apply this to our daily lives. We all have needs of one kind or another. What do we do with our needs? Where can we find help in time of need? I love the words of the writer of **Hebrews in 4:16**.

"Let us therefore draw near with confidence to the throne of grace, that we may receive

mercy and may find grace to help in time of need." (NAS)

The water flows forth from the throne. All good things come down from above. My friend and brother or sister in Christ, go to God with all your problems, needs, and fears. Help comes from the throne of grace.

On both sides of the River of Life, and between the two lanes of the street, runs a line of trees, called the Tree of Life, bearing twelve varieties of fruit, and producing this fruit every month. We will discuss this in greater detail later, but one thing stands out here in stark contrast to our normal conception of time in eternity. This fruit is produced every month, and there are 12 types of fruit. What does this tell us about time in the New Jerusalem? There will be months. Will the trees yield a crop of one variety each month for 12 months? This would suggest a yearly cycle. However, it could be that the trees will yield 12 varieties of fruit at a time, producing this fruit monthly. Scripture is not clear on this matter. At any rate it is clear that some type of monthly cycle will take place. Yet there will be no night there, just daytime all the time, **Revelation 21:25**. How the month will be regulated, we do not know. Will God return the new universe to a similar program as at the present one, with the sun and moon, plus the rotation of the new earth providing the changes necessary to regulate time? We'll understand it better by and by.

Its Temple

"And I saw no temple in the city, for its temple is the Lord God the Almighty and the Lamb." (Revelation 21:22 RSV)

Have you ever been to a city where there was not a single church? When we say that it is unchurched, we imply that the city is full of unsaved people without true Christian believers, or very few of them. Not so this city. The New Jerusalem is one giant temple. The throne of God and the Lamb is in it, so God is ever present there. There is no need for a separate building or buildings that we call church, or for a house-church as in the days of the early church. There will be no pastors, no pulpits, no hymn books, no church committees, no building programs, no church bulletins, no pot-luck dinners - all the props and equipment we find so necessary today will be gone. Then again will be fulfilled the millennial words of the Lord to Jeremiah, as quoted in **Hebrews 8:11**.

"And they shall not teach everyone his fellow citizen, and everyone his brother, saying, 'Know the Lord,' for all shall know me, from the least to the greatest of them." (NAS)

Its Light

The book of Genesis records the creation of light before the sun had been made and placed in its orbit. In fact, the very first creative act of God, after He had made the heavens and the earth, was to create light, and divide the light from the darkness on the first day in Genesis 1. It wasn't until the fourth day that God made the sun. For three days the earth was filled with light that did not come from the sun above.

Now once again in the New Jerusalem there will be light from another source besides the sun. Listen to the words of John in **Revelation 21:23-24**.

"The city has no need of the sun or of the moon to shine on it, because God's glory illumines it and the Lamb is its light. By its light the nations will walk and to it the kings of the earth will bring their splendor." (ML)

The glory of God and the Lamb provide abundant light for this wonderful city. This was prophesied in the Old Testament by *Isaiah 60:19-20* as pertaining to the glorified Mt. Zion.

"No longer will you have the sun for light by day, nor for brightness will the moon give you light. But you will have the Lord for an everlasting light, and your God for your glory. Your sun will set no more; neither will your moon wane; for you will have the Lord for an everlasting light." (NAS)

What light is this? Is it the Shekinah glory of God once again as He appeared in the cloud by day and pillar of fire by night to lead the children of Israel to the Promised Land? The Lamb is again mentioned here as providing light. It is interesting that even here, Christ's mission on earth is not forgotten. He is the Lamb of God who came to take away this world's sin, by bearing it on his own body on the Cross. He is the eternal Lamb. His mission on earth is remembered forever.

What does light symbolize? Light speaks of holiness, just like darkness speaks of sin. The God of this world, Satan, darkens the mind of the unbelievers so that the light of the Gospel of Christ will not penetrate into their darkened mind, *2 Corinthians 4:4*. Light also speaks of understanding, of the light dawning in one's mind, of being able to grasp a spiritual concept. In his first epistle, this same writer, the apostle John, states that God is light. And James makes the following statement:

"Every good thing bestowed, and every perfect gift is from above, coming down from the Father of Lights, with whom there is no variation, or shifting shadow." (James 1:17 NAS)

God is the Father of lights. What does this mean? What or who are the lights? The Greek word for light cannot be applied only to the heavenly lights, as the NIV translates it, since it is the same word used for the light of Christ, the light of the Gospel. It could have a wide range of meanings. Let me list a few.

1. He is the Father of physical light, having created light, the sun and moon and stars - All the heavenly bodies.

2. Taken figuratively, he is the Father of goodness and wisdom.

3. It could refer to the Shekinah Glory of God in the Old Testament, the light that led the Children of Israel and then manifested itself in the tabernacle and temple.

4. Spiritually, He is the Father of grace and glory, of holiness and spiritual understanding.

5. Ecclesiastically, He is the Father of every true believer in His church. Christ Himself stated that His children are the light of the world, and so should shine as lights in the darkness of sin.

Ellicott's Commentary on the Whole Bible states that Bishop Wordsworth, many years ago, wrote the following words:

"God is the Father of all lights, the light of the natural world, the sun, the moon and stars, shining in the heavens; the light of reason and conscience; the light of His law; the light of prophecy, shining in a dark place; the light of the Gospel shining throughout the world; the light of the apostles, confessors, martyrs, bishops, and priests, preaching the Gospel to all nations, the light of the Holy Spirit, shining in our hearts; the light of the heavenly city - God is the Father of them all. He is the everlasting Father of the everlasting Son, who is the Light of the World."

To this we can say a resounding AMEN!

THE FATHER OF LIGHTS

The Father of Lights in heaven above
  Abundant blessing bestows.
He gives good things and perfect gifts
  To those He eternally knows.

"Don't be deceived," he speaks to His flock,
  "I never tempt any man;
No evil I send to my people in need,
  It's just not a part of my plan."

The Father of Lights looks down on the earth,
  Filled with darkness of sin and despair,
Watching thousands of lights scattered all through the land,
  For He lit them with tender care,

What are these lights shining over the world,
  Providing such brilliant sights?
They're disciples of Christ, the Light of the world,
  For God is the Father of Lights.

HE

I would like to quote one more verse along this line. It is Malachi 4:2a.

"But for you who fear my name the sun of righteousness will rise with healing in its wings." (NAS)

In the New Jerusalem, the Son is the sun. He comes with healing in His wings. The light of that glorious city will not be sunlight but Sonlight. If Dr. Kellog's theory of the re-canopied earth, previously mentioned, is true, which seems quite logical to me, and the earth with the New Jerusalem is enclosed in a canopy of some kind, the light of that city will be internal, flowing out from the presence of God and the Lamb.

The New Jerusalem, God's eternal city, the "mountain of the house of the Lord" will be fifteen hundred miles long, fifteen hundred miles wide, and fifteen hundred miles high to its peak, surrounded by a 216 foot high wall, and built on twelve foundation stones. I picture it as in the illustration below.

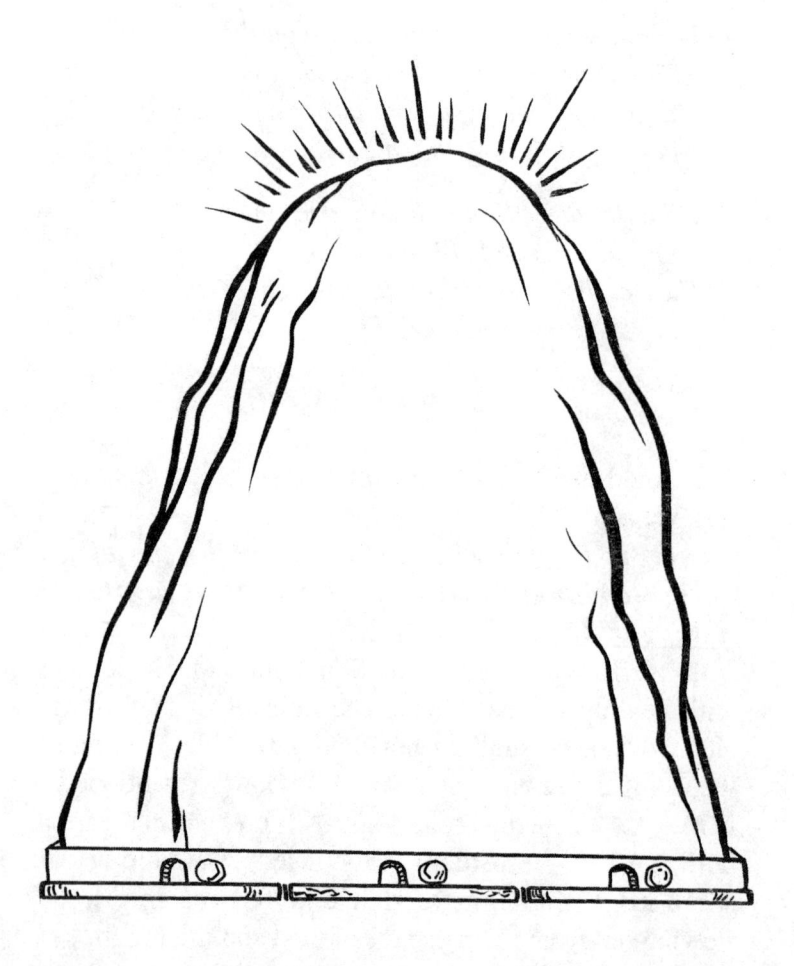

A Closer Look

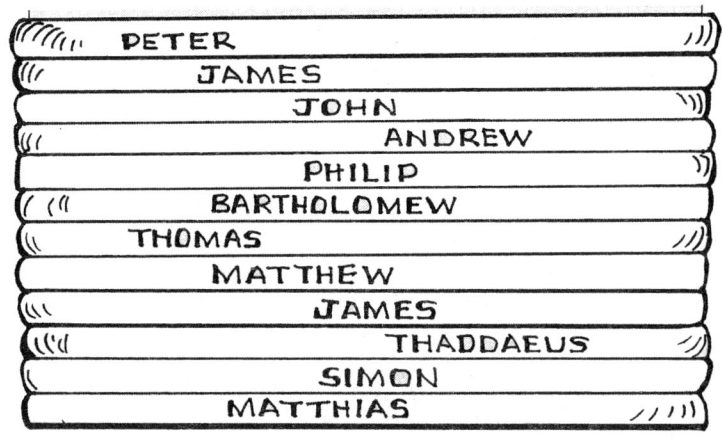

```
PETER
JAMES
JOHN
ANDREW
PHILIP
BARTHOLOMEW
THOMAS
MATTHEW
JAMES
THADDAEUS
SIMON
MATTHIAS
```

The illustration above and below represent two possible interpretations of the 216 foot wall that will surround the New Jerusalem. Some Bible teachers envision three foundation stones under each of the four walls, while others see twelve layers of foundation stones around the wall.

The New Jerusalem's street of gold will evidently be a wide boulevard with the river of life flowing through the middle of it and the tree of life growing on both banks of the river, as in the illustration below.

PART 4

THE PEOPLE OF THE NEW JERUSALEM

Most of us prefer living where there are other people. Have you ever been to a ghost town? Deserted, abandoned, with unpainted, broken-down buildings, half-hinged shutters clanging wildly in the wind. Scary! A ghost town is not a preferred place to live, certainly not on the list of the ten most popular places. We naturally want to be with people, and not just any people, but friendly people, interesting people, and people with whom we can establish a friendship and spend enjoyable times in discussion, sharing our experiences and listening to theirs.

And so as we take a closer look inside the New Jerusalem, the eternal city of God, we want to know who we will spend eternity with. What will they be like? What will we be like? What will we do? Scripture gives us many insights into the glorious life that awaits us.

Chapter Seven
Who Will Be There?

There are evidently two groups of people who will have access to this great city. One group will actually live in the New Jerusalem as its citizens, while the second group will have access to the New Jerusalem for visits. Where do I get this strange teaching? I hasten to explain.

The Citizens of the New Jerusalem.

The Lord Jesus made a startling promise to his disciples before his death on the Cross. Listen to His words.

"In my Father's house are many dwelling places; if it were not so, I would have told you; for I go to prepare a place for you. And if I go and prepare a place for you, I will come again, and receive you to Myself, that where I am, there you may be also." (John 14:2-3 NAS)

The old King James version uses the word "mansions" instead of "dwelling places". The NIV calls them rooms. Christ ascended into heaven nearly 2,000 years ago. Can you imagine what a beautiful place He has been preparing for us ever since! The hymn writer gloried in this blessed hope, while writing the following words:

I've got a mansion just over the hilltop.
In that bright land where we'll never grow old.
Then someday yonder, we will never more wander,
But walk on streets that are purest gold.

> *Don't think me poor, or deserted or lonely.*
> *I'm not discouraged, I'm heaven bound.*
> *I'm just a pilgrim in search of a city,*
> *I want a mansion, a harp and a crown.*
>
> Ira Stanphill

But to some people the idea of a having a beautiful mansion is too much. Their desires are not nearly so lofty. They sing:

Many years I've been looking for a place to call home,
But I've failed here to find it, so I must travel on;
I don't care for fine mansions on earth's sinking sand,
Lord, build me a cabin in the corner of glory land.

Yes, build me just a cabin in the corner of glory land
In the shade of the Tree of Life that it may ever stand.
Where I can just hear the angels sing, and shake Jesus hand.
Lord, build me a cabin in the corner of glory land.

> Cpl. Curtis Stewart

Both of these songs were printed in Heart-Warming Songs No. 2.

Whether a mansion or a cabin, it makes very little difference, actually. We will be so taken up with our Lord and so awed by the amazing things we will see and experience that our dwelling place will be all of Paradise. Some people imagine that the type of house we will inhabit there depends on our service for Christ here on earth.

The story is told, whether true or not, I do not know, about a wealthy lady who dreamed that she died and went to heaven. There she met saint Peter, who showed her around the glorious place. They passed a beautiful mansion, and she immediately inquired if that would be her house. "No," replied Peter, "actually that place belongs to your maid. She was a good follower of Christ and that is her reward." This made her even more anxious to take a look at her own mansion, so Peter led her to another part of Paradise and pointed to a little shack. "This is your house," he said. She was taken aback, and replied to Peter: "But I-I-I thought I would have a beautiful mansion, even better than my maid's." "No," responded Peter, "We did the very best we could with the materials you sent over here, but you didn't send very much and they were not of good quality, so this is all we could come up with."

Now actually, that was just a dream, and though it gives us something to think about, the idea of our eternal home being built with materials we send on ahead has no basis in Scripture. There will be rewards, as we have already seen. However, what Christ means by "dwelling place" is unclear. We do not know if we will have individual homes, or if by dwelling place He is referring to the many unbelievably beautiful sites and scenes in the New Jerusalem. What need will we have for a mansion or a cabin with the new spiritual bodies we will inhabit anyway? This is not to say that we will not have individual places of residence, but simply that we do not know. Since we are accustomed to houses here on earth, it may be that God will actually provide individual homes for us there.

Let's take another look at *Revelation 21:2-3* and *21:10.*

"And I saw the holy city, new Jerusalem, coming down out of heaven from God, made ready as a bride adorned for her husband. And I heard a loud voice from the throne, saying, 'Behold, the tabernacle of God is among men, and He shall dwell among them, and they shall

be His people, and God Himself shall be among them." (NAS)

"And he carried me away in the Spirit to a great and high mountain, and showed me the holy city, Jerusalem, coming down out of heaven from God." (NAS)

Who will live in the New Jerusalem? The bride or wife of Christ. While the church is said to be the bride of Christ in the New Testament, *Ephesians 5:22-27*, the Old Testament points to the Children of Israel as the wife of Jehovah, *Isaiah 54:5-7*. There are a number of Scripture verses that link the Old Testament Jehovah with the New Testament Jesus as one and the same. Check out *Isaiah 6:1* and *10* with *John 12:36b-41*. It would seem that "the saints of all the ages will be there," as the song goes. That the church of Christ, composed of all true believers from the day of Pentecost until the Rapture, will live there is clearly indicated in *Hebrews 12:22-23* in these words to the church:

"But you have come to Mount Zion, to the heavenly Jerusalem, the city of the living God. You have come to thousands upon thousands of angels in joyful assembly, to the church of the firstborn, whose names are written in heaven." (NIV)

And then there are the Old Testament saints. Hebrews 11 tells about their desire for this heavenly city. Abraham "was looking for the city which has foundations, whose architect and builder is God." *(vs. 10 NAS)* All these "make it clear that they are seeking a country of their own... a heavenly one. Therefore God is not ashamed to be called their God, for He has prepared a city for them." *(vs. 14-16 NAS)*

The fact that the names of the twelve tribes of Israel are on the gates of the city indicate the presence of Old Testament saints there as well.

Three figures are used to describe those who will reside in that City of God.

The pre-registered.

Those who are enrolled in heaven, having their names in the Lamb's Book of Life, when they accepted Christ as their Savior.

"And nothing unclean and no one who practices abomination and lying, shall ever come into it, but only those whose names are written in the Lamb's book of life." (Revelation 21:27 NAS)

The overcomers.

This is not a special group of Christians, but refers to all of God's people. All are overcomers to some degree, and none are total or perfect overcomers.

"He who overcomes shall inherit these things, and I will be his God and he will be My son. (Revelation 21:7 NAS)

How does one become an overcomer? There is an old story that I heard only once in my lifetime, back while I was attending Prairie Bible Institute in Alberta, Canada. I have a hard time believing that it is true. Probably just another one of those stories that pastors sometimes tell, invented stories, perhaps something like a parable, that has a good lesson to teach. Now with all that introduction, here is the story.

A young pastor began his first ministry in a little country church with certain forebodings, as all beginning ministers do. Fortunately, he had a good friend who pastored a large church in the city and had a lot of experience in the pastorate. Whenever this young pastor had a problem that he could not solve, he would invariably send a letter to his experienced friend in the city and ask for his advice. Things would go well for a while again until another problem came up. On one of those occasions he wrote to the older pastor of the large city church to ask his counsel about a sticky issue that the church was facing. The older pastor received the letter, and sat down to write him a reply. It so happened that he also wrote a letter to the administrator of a ranch he owned out in the country, and, by mistake, placed the letter to his administrator in the envelope addressed to the young minister. When the young pastor got the letter, he was puzzled by its contents. He couldn't seem to understand it. Over and over he read it. Then it occurred to him that his friend was sending his advice in the form of a parable. So he began to study the parable to locate its teachings. He found three points in the counsel from the older and wiser pastor. The first suggestion was to cut the grass. "Perhaps that means that I should suppress those personal sins and those of the congregation that spring up from our own sinful nature. Keep them mowed down," he thought. The second point was to mend the fences. "Ah! That must refer to my need to keep the spiritual fences repaired so that the influence of the world will not enter and damage the church." In the third place, the pastor told him to watch out for the old black bull. "How important to keep my eye on Satan and his tactics!" thought the young pastor. Well, he followed the advice and again the church prospered.

Yes! What good advice! We all can and should overcome the temptations of the enemy to a greater degree than we do. Tell me, are you keeping the grass (weeds) cut in your life? How about the fences? Are they in good repair and keeping out the invasions of the world with all its allures? And what about Satan, our arch enemy? Are you aware of his tactics, his methods of operation, the temptations that he personalizes to your areas of weakness? I love the words of *Revelation 12:11* concerning the way to be an overcomer. It states:

"And they overcame him by the blood of the Lamb and by the word of their testimony, and they did not love their lives to the death." (NKJ)

The washed.

"Blessed are those who wash their robes, that they may have the right to the tree of life, and may enter by the gates into the city." (Revelation 22:14 NAS)

"...and he said to me, 'These are the ones who come out of the great tribulation, and they have washed their robes and made them white in the blood of the Lamb." (Revelation 7:14 NAS)

"Or do you not know that the unrighteous shall not inherit the kingdom of God? Do not be deceived; neither fornicators, nor idolaters, nor adulterers, nor effeminate, nor homosexuals, nor thieves, nor the covetous, nor drunkards, nor revilers, nor swindlers shall inherit the kingdom of God. And such were some of you; but you were washed, but you were sanctified, but you were justified in the name of the Lord Jesus Christ, and in the Spirit of our God." (1 Cor. 6:9-11 NAS)

This is the third characteristic of those who will actually live in the New Jerusalem. They have been washed of all their sin stains. This reminds me of an incident that took place in a little town called Campo Alegre, far up the Caura River in Venezuela. I believe that it is the last Venezuelan settlement along the Caura River before getting into Indian country. We tied up our launch alongside several dugout canoes and walked several miles into the village. As we approached the first homes, the church bell began to ring, advising the people of our coming. We were holding services in the little chapel there, when, at the close of one of the services, a man who was very evidently under the influence of liquor came up from the back and said in Spanish: "Yo quiero meterme evangelico. Iniciame, pues. Iniciame." Translated it means: "I want to become an evangelical. Initiate me. Initiate me." He wanted us to perform some sort of ceremony that would automatically make an evangelical out of him. However, one does not become a Christian by means of any ceremony or rite, not even by the church. Access to the kingdom of God comes by receiving Christ as Savior from sin. When one takes this step of faith, his name is written in the Lamb's Book of Life, his sins are washed away, and he becomes an overcomer. Is this your experience? It can be, if you will only bow your head and ask Jesus to come into your life as your Savior and Lord. Do it now.

The Visitors to the New Jerusalem

The Old Testament and New Testament saints will not be the only people in that renewed earth. John goes on to talk about others in *Revelation 21:24-27*.

"The nations will walk by its light, and the kings of the earth will bring their splendor into it. On no day will its gates ever be shut, for there

will be no night there. The glory and honor of the nations will be brought into it." (NIV)

Then will be fulfilled the words of *Psalm 72:11*.

"And let all kings bow down before him. All nations serve him." (NAS)

Yes, there will be nations and kings there on that day. The word nations is "ethne" in Greek, from which we get the word ethnic. It is not necessarily speaking of nations as we now know them, and certainly not the nations of today, but it really means ethnic groups or peoples. But where do these people groups come from. If the Old Testament saints are not living in the New Jerusalem, for some think that only the church is the bride of Christ and will have this privileged place, though I do not agree with them; but if so, then the multitudes of Jewish believers, who like Abraham, were justified by faith and not works, will occupy the earth. But even without the Old Testament believers, there will still be a vast multitude, composed of the saints of the Great Tribulation period, most if not all who have been martyred for their faith in Christ, plus the hundreds of thousands who have gone through the Millennium, the thousand year reign of Christ, when there will be no war, famine or plague, and with very long life once again, during which time they will continue to bear children. All these groups would make up a vast number of people to populate the renovated earth. These will form themselves into nations or ethnic groups. They will have kings over them. Who will the kings be? Let's look at some more verses of Scripture to find the answer.

"But the saints of the most High shall take the kingdom, and possess the kingdom for ever; even for ever and ever." (Daniel 7:18 KJ)

> *"And the kingdom and dominion, and the greatness of the kingdom under the whole heaven, shall be given unto the people of the saints of the most High, whose kingdom is an everlasting kingdom, and all dominions shall serve and obey Him." (Daniel 7:27 KJ)*
>
> *"Jesus said to them, 'Truly, I say to you, in the new world, when the Son of man shall sit on his glorious throne, you who have followed me will also sit on twelve thrones, judging the twelve tribes of Israel.'" (Matthew 19:28 RSV)*
>
> *"...the throne of God and of the Lamb shall be in it, and His bondservants shall serve Him...and they shall reign forever and ever." (Revelation 22:3b,5b NAS)*

The Daniel verse claims that the saints of God will receive a kingdom forever. In this context these saints would likely be Jewish believers who will reign with Christ over the earth. Christ's words in **Matthew 19:28** could be referring to the Millennium, instead of the eternal state, since the word "world" is often translated "age". This reign will extend into eternity. The promise in **Revelation 22:3-5** is quite clear that the bondservants of Christ will reign on the earth. It would appear then that the kings of these nations will be taken from the apostles and the Old and New Testament followers of Christ.

What does "the glory of the nations" refer to in **Revelation 21:24** and **26?** Let's take a look at these verses.

> *"And the nations shall walk by its light, and the kings of the earth shall bring their glory into it...And they shall bring the glory and the honor of the nations into it." (NAS)*

A look at such verses as **_Esther 1:1-4, Isaiah 35:1-2,_** and **_Isaiah 60:13_** show us that the beauty and riches of the nations are being referred to here. These will be taken to the New Jerusalem to honor and glorify God and the Lamb, just as the Queen of Sheba took the best of her kingdom to King Solomon.

It is true that we are given very few details about the things that will be there in this beautiful city, in the renovated earth, and in the new heavens. We are not told if there will be stars and planets in the heavens, animals of any kind here on earth, about the presence of flowers and trees besides the Tree of Life, about food apart from the Tree of Life, about means of travel, about sleep, and about a host of other things that we presently know and enjoy. This does not necessarily mean that they are absent. Many things are left to our imagination. However, the New Jerusalem and new earth contain so many things that we are familiar with, (wall, street, river, trees, fruit, precious stones, people, nations, kings, light) that very likely many of the other things that we now enjoy will also be there, even though they are not mentioned. One of my favorite verses is **_Psalm 16:11_**.

"Thou wilt make known to me the path of life; in Thy presence is fullness of joy; in Thy right hand there are pleasures forevermore." (NAS)

Chapter Eight
What Will We Be Like?

There is not a lot of Scripture describing the body we will have when we get to the New Jerusalem, but there is some information, especially in *1 Corinthians 15:35-54*, about our resurrected bodies. From this passage we gather the following conclusions:

Our bodies will be resurrected and transformed. The resurrection of the dead is the subject of this whole chapter, as Paul seeks to prove that there will be such a resurrection. In vs. 35 he states:

"But someone will say, 'How are the dead raised? And with what kind of body do they come?'" (NAS)

This is the question of this chapter. What will we be like? What will our new bodies be like? Paul goes on to show in the following verses that a great change will take place in our bodies at the resurrection. When a grain of wheat is planted, it emerges with a completely different body, though coming from the grain. Just like seeds differ in size and appearance, like the flesh of people and animals differs, like the heavenly bodies differ in their appearance and glory, so the resurrected body will differ from the one we now live in. There is a sense in which it will be the same body, or at least the same person, because this will be a resurrection, not a new creation. Let's look at this further explanation in vss. 50-53.

"Now I say this brethren, that flesh and blood cannot inherit the kingdom of God; nor does the per-

ishable inherit the imperishable. Behold, I tell you a mystery; we shall not all sleep but we shall all be changed, in a moment, in the twinkling of an eye, at the last trumpet; for the trumpet will sound, and the dead will be raised imperishable, and we shall be changed. For this perishable must put on the imperishable, and this mortal must put on immortality."
(1 Corinthians 15:50-53 NAS)

Our bodies will be resurrected and transformed. That which is perishable will be made imperishable, so that no disease, decay, or deterioration will ever be able to set in. The new body will be raised in glory and power, now a spiritual body rather than a merely physical body. Just as we have lived inside an earthly body of flesh and bones, so we will live in a heavenly body that will be immortal. Our new bodies will be like Christ's resurrected body. This is Paul's conclusion in vss. 45-49. We were made like Adam, the first man, and at the resurrection will be made like Christ, the second man who is from heaven. The beloved apostle John concurs with this in *1 John 3:2.*

"Beloved, now we are children of God, and it has not appeared as yet what we shall be. We know that, when He appears, we shall be like Him, because we shall see Him just as He is." (NAS)

Many years before the Psalmist penned words rather similar to these.

"As for me, with righteousness shall I behold Thy face. I shall be satisfied when I awake with Thy likeness." (Psalm 17:15 ML)

Other verses that you may want to look up along this line are *2 Corinthians 4:14 and 5:1-10*. Not only will we be able to see Christ as He really is in all His glory, but we will be transformed and changed into His image to be like Him. I love the words of the apostle Paul in *Philippians 3:20-21*:

"But our citizenship is in heaven. And we eagerly await a Savior from there, the Lord Jesus Christ, who, by the power that enables him to bring everything under his control, will transform our lowly bodies so that they will be like his glorious body." (NIV)

What was Christ's resurrected body like?

Christ's resurrected body was composed of flesh and bones. When Christ appeared to His disciples after His resurrection, they were startled and frightened. He immediately reassured them with these words:

"Why are you troubled, and why do doubts rise in your minds? Look at my hands and my feet. It is I myself! Touch me and see; a ghost does not have flesh and bones, as you see I have." (Luke 24:38-39 NIV)

The tomb was empty. Christ Himself was raised from the dead and came out of the tomb. It was His own body, His own hands, and His own feet. He could be seen, heard, and touched. He was not an eerie ghost or specter, floating around. The statement in *1 Corinthains 15:50* that "flesh and blood shall not inherit the kingdom of God," does not contradict this. "Flesh and blood" is different than "flesh and bones". Christ shed His blood on Calvary's Cross. The physical life is in the blood. Our new bodies, like Christ's new body, will not be nourished by a bloodstream, as at the present time. It will be a spiritual body not a physical body, with the Holy Spirit filling and nourishing it. The ancient and long-suffering Job had this hope. Listen to his words in *Job 19:25-27*.

" I know that my Redeemer lives, and that in the end he will stand upon the earth. And after

my skin has been destroyed, yet in my flesh I will see God; I myself will see him with my own eyes - I, and not another." (NIV)

His faith was firm. God had somehow revealed to him that in the end time he will stand on this earth, and he is sure that at that time in his flesh he will see God. So we will have flesh. Not the same kind as we have now, subject to boils, corns, blisters, sunburn, and diseases of all kinds. No, this will be glorified, transformed flesh, free from the weaknesses and frailties of our present body.

The new body will evidently be freed from physical restraints. Since it will be like Christ's body, let's look at some Scripture that gives us an idea of what that was like.

"And their eyes were opened and they recognized Him, and He vanished from their sight." (Luke 24:31 NAS)

"When therefore it was evening, on that day, the first day of the week, and when the doors were shut where the disciples were, for fear of the Jews, Jesus came and stood in their midst, and said to them, 'Peace be with you.'" (John 20:19 NAS)

"And after eight days again His disciples were inside, and Thomas with them, Jesus came, the doors having been shut, and stood in their midst, and said, 'Peace be with you.'" (John 20:26 NAS)

"And while they were telling these things, He Himself stood in their midst." (Luke 24:36 NAS)

"And while they still could not believe it for joy and were marveling, He said to them, 'Have you anything here to eat?' And they gave

What Will We Be Like?

Him a piece of broiled fish; and He took it and ate it before them." (Luke 24:41-43 NAS)

Jesus was able to appear and disappear, vanishing into thin air before the startled eyes of the awe struck disciples. He could enter a room without opening the door, and he could eat. After all, He did promise to eat the fruit of the vine again with His disciples in the Kingdom of God. Our bodies will be like His glorious body. Of course, one could make a case that He was able to do all this because of His deity, and since we will never attain deity, we may not be able to do these things. I prefer to believe that He did what we also will be able to do, but if I'm wrong, don't come and say you told me so on that day. Will we be able to fly? Will we travel from one place to another by a miracle of transportation - just to disappear and appear at another place? Like Phillip did after he baptized the Ethiopian eunuch. One would think so! That will be an amazing day!

In **Revelation 21:4** we are given a further glimpse into our life at that time. It states:

"He will wipe every tear from their eyes. There will be no more death or mourning or crying or pain, for the old order of things has passed away." (NIV)

In our glorified bodies we will never be sick again. No colds or flu to bother us; none of the many allergies that make life miserable for so many; no cancer, heart attacks, strokes, or diseases of any kind. We will enjoy perfect health. Wonderful! Those of God's saints whose bodies have been wracked with pain throughout much of their life have the glorious hope of a pain-free body forever. The exclusion of pain from our eternal existence also excludes the possibilities of falls, accidents, cuts, bee stings, etc., etc. No crying from pain. No mourning at the death of loved ones. For no one will die. The glorified body is made for life, life abundant and life eternal.

While we are looking into what we will be like on that eternal day, we should check the words of Christ in *Matthew 22:30* as He responds to the question of the Sadducees about marriage after the resurrection.

"At the resurrection people will neither marry nor be given in marriage; they will be like the angels in heaven." (NIV)

Those of us who enjoy married life may not be too happy with this information. However, there is no doubt that we will be so taken up with Jesus and the eternal bliss we will enjoy, that the thought of marriage or the need for marriage, will never cross our minds. We will be like the angels in heaven. Now, hold on! Does that infer that we will be able to fly like they can? Or does this refer only to marriage? You decide.

Chapter Nine
Will We Know Each Other?

That's another question. Will we recognize each other? Scripture indicates that the answer to this question is affirmative, that we will know and recognize each other. One verse stands out, but there are others that we will also look at. First, check out *1 Corinthians 13:12*.

"For now we see in a mirror dimly, but then face to face; now I know in part, but then I shall know fully just as I also have been fully known." (NAS)

Let's analyze this promise.

"I shall know fully as I have been fully know."

By whom have I been fully known? By other people? My friends and family already know me. I also know them now. But this knowledge is partial. We do not know each other fully.

By God? Certainly. He is the only one who fully knows me. In *1 Corinthians 8:3* Paul writes:

"But if anyone loves God, he is known by Him." (NAS)

Conclusion: We shall know as we are known by God.

What shall we know? Facts, information, things, or people? People, since we are people whom God knows.

Conclusion: We shall know other people as we are known by God.

How does God know us? Fully. The Good Shepherd knows His sheep. Will we know others fully? Probably not, because only God knows everything. He alone is omniscient. The Bible says He knows everything, because He is Creator and Lord and knows everything through his omniscience. The verse likely means that in the same way as God knows us, we will know each other.

How did God get to know you? When did God get acquainted with you? There was a time when you met God, if you are a born again Christian, but God knew you long before that. God knows all things and all people, present, past, and future. God knows intuitively. In the same way we shall intuitively know others. Intuitively.

Conclusion: We shall know others intuitively just as God knows us.

Now let's look at some other verses that testify to the truth of this statement - that we will know each other intuitively. In other words we will know without having had to be introduced or learn about them in some way.

"And behold Moses and Elijah appeared to them, talking with Him. (Matthew 17:3 NAS)

How did Matthew and the disciples know that these two men were Moses and Elijah? They certainly had never met them. They had never seen a picture of them. Christ did not stop to introduce them. They must have know intuitively by the inner voice of God.

"But being full of the Holy Spirit, he gazed intently into heaven and saw the glory of God, and Jesus standing at the right hand of God." (Acts 7:55 NAS)

How did Stephen know it was Jesus standing there? Had he ever seen Him? Possibly. Perhaps not. We do not know. But he knew it was Jesus. He just knew.

> *"And I say to you, that many shall come from east and west, and recline at the table with Abraham, and Isaac, and Jacob in the kingdom of heaven."* *(Matthew 8:11 NAS)*

How will we know that the three men there are Abraham, Isaac, and Jacob. We will just know. We will know intuitively.

> *"But now he has died; why should I fast? Can I bring him back again? I shall go to him, but he will not return to me."* *(2 Samuel 12:23 NAS)*

These were the words of David after the death of his baby who was born to Bathsheba. "I shall go to him." This is our hope too. Those of us who have lost children to death believe that some day we will see them again. We shall go to them. We will know them and they will know us. Intuitively. God will give us this knowledge.

My wife Helen and I are looking forward to seeing and getting to know our son David in that heavenly kingdom. We never had a chance to get to know him. The Lord had graciously given us three healthy sons, all born in Venezuela, but the fourth one was another story. David was born at about six months and eight days, and lived just twelve hours. He had been oxygen-starved, and probably had severe brain damage, so in a way it was a blessing that the Lord took him home. I almost lost my wife Helen also, as her blood pressure plummeted way too low, and she needed a quick blood transfusion. We are forever grateful to a member of a local church, who immediately went to the hospital and donated blood for her. You can imagine that it was a sad day, when I buried little David in the cemetery behind the hospital. I called a pastor friend to accompany me, but he was not available. Helen was still in the hospital. A hospital employee and

I stood alone by the gravesite, while I read from the Scripture and prayed to commend little David to the Lord. We firmly believe that someday we will see him again in that eternal city of God. We will know him intuitively.

James B. Singleton wrote a beautiful song way back in 1956 that, in my humble opinion, is a classic, and should live through the ages. It is called:

I will not be a stranger.

I will not be a stranger when I get to that city;
I'm acquainted with folks over there.
There'll be friends there to greet me,
There'll be loved ones to meet me,
At the gates of that city foursquare.

Thru the years, thru the tears, they have gone one by one,
But they'll wait at the gate, until my race is run.
I will not be a stranger when I get to that city,
I'm acquainted with folks over there.

I will not be a stranger when I get to that city,
I've a home on those streets paved with gold;
I will feel right at home there
In that beautiful "Somewhere,"
With my loved ones whose mem'ries I hold.

I will not be a stranger when I get to that city,
There'll be no lonely days over there;
There'll be no stormy weather
But a great get together,
On the streets of that city foursquare.

It does appear, however, that we will not remember the things that happened in this life. The prophet Isaiah speaks thus in 65:17.

"For behold, I create new heavens and a new earth; and the former things shall not be remembered or come to mind." (NAS)

Many jokes are constantly circulating about our forgetfulness, especially as we grow older. I like the one about the pastor who, while visiting one of his elderly parishioners, asked the question: "Do you ever think about the hereafter?" She quickly replied: "Pastor, I'm always thinking about the hereafter. Every time I go into another room, I ask myself: Now what am I here after?"

The one I like the best has to do with two senior citizens who were having trouble remembering things. One day she said to him: "Henry, go to the store and buy us some bread and milk. But write it down, Henry, because if you don't, you'll forget it for sure." "That's easy to remember," answered Henry. "Bread and milk, I won't forget." And so off went Henry to the store without writing it down. Along the way, just as his wife had said, he forgot what she wanted. "No problem," he said to himself. "I'll just walk up and down the aisles until I come to what she wants, and then I'll remember." As he walked the aisles, he came to the Dairy Section. "That's it!" he muttered. "She wants ice cream." So he picked out a half gallon of vanilla ice cream. "Now, what would go with ice cream? Cookies!" Henry selected a box of cookies, paid for his purchase, and headed home. "Here it is, Honey," he shouted to his wife. She came to him, opened the shopping bag, looked at the vanilla ice cream and cookies, and exclaimed: "Oh, Henry, you did too forget. I wanted chocolate."

Forgetting is not always a blessing at the present time, although even now there are things that we would be better off if we forgot. What about our hurts and our past sins? Even past blessings should not be held onto too long, as we need new blessings daily. However, to be able to totally forget the past on that day will be a great blessing, especially for those who have suffered a lot here below, either physically with a body wracked by pain, or emotionally as they have lived under difficult circumstances. It is often a blessing to forget. We need to have good forgetters. It is great that God remembers our sin no more. We also will be able to forget all the heartaches and pain caused by our sin, all the times we disobeyed and displeased God, all the lost opportunities to serve Him. As He wipes all tears from our eyes, He will also give us the ability to forget the past. How could we enjoy our heavenly home if we carried around with us the memories of these sinful days on earth? God will allow us to forget. I am convinced of that.

Chapter Ten
What Will We Do?

Will we float around on white billowy clouds and strum our harps? I wouldn't mind doing that for awhile. But just for awhile. God is a God of infinite variety, having created so many species of animals and plants, sea life and birds of the air, people of many races and colors with different personalities and appearances. No doubt He has planned an infinite variety of activities for those He takes with him to that celestial city, come down to earth. There are at least four activities mentioned in Scripture that we will participate in.

We will serve Christ in person, face to face, and reign with Him.

> *"No longer will there be any curse. The throne of God and of the Lamb will be in the city, and his servants will serve him. They will see his face, and his name will be on their foreheads. There will be no more night. They will not need the light of a lamp or the light of the sun, for the Lord God will give them light. And they will reign forever and ever. (Revelation 22:3-5 NIV)*

Christ will be King of Kings and Lord of Lords in that day, sharing the throne of His Father. We will see Him face to face, and will serve Him in whatever He desires of us, for we will reign with Him over the renewed earth. Listen to the promise that Jesus made to His twelve disciples while He still walked among them.

> *"Truly I say to you, that you who have followed Me, in the regeneration when the Son of Man will sit on His glorious throne, you also shall sit upon twelve thrones, judging the twelve tribes of Israel." (Matthew 19:28 NAS)*

This could well refer to the time of the Millennium, when Christ rules for a thousand years with a rod of iron. Will the twelve tribes of Israel, as a distinct national entity, go into eternity? If so, then the twelve disciples will sit on thrones as their judges. Now let's take a look at what Paul says to the Corinthian Christians regarding the lofty position and privilege of the church of Christ.

> *"Or do you not know that the saints will judge the world? And if the world is judged by you, are you not competent to constitute the smallest law courts? Do you not know that we shall judge angels? (1 Corinthians 6:2-3a NAS)*

What all this will entail only God knows. Saints like the Corinthian Christians, like you and me, will have the awesome privilege of sitting as judges over the world, and even over angels. Wow! We will take our orders direct from Christ as we stand in His presence, and will go out to judge and reign over those He puts under our guidance.

We will sing and worship God.

The book of Revelation is filled with songs of adoration to God. Wonderful songs. Short songs. Perhaps we should call them choruses. Some are sung and some are recited. Read through the following songs and let the Holy Spirit lift your heart in praise and adoration to Almighty God and His Son, the Lamb.

The four living creatures say :
"Holy, holy, holy is the Lord God Almighty, who was, and is, and is to come." (4:8 NIV)

The twenty four elders fall prostrate before the throne of God, placing their crowns at His feet, and worship Him, saying:
"You are worthy, our Lord and God, to receive glory and honor and power, for you created all things, and by your will they were created and have their being." (4:11 NIV)

The four living creatures and twenty-four elders sing a new song:
"You are worthy to take the scroll and to open its seals, because you were slain, and with your blood you purchased men for God from every tribe and language and people and nation. You have made them to be a kingdom and priests to serve our God, and they will reign on the earth." (5:9-10 NIV)

Millions of angels encircling the throne sing:
"Worthy is the Lamb, who was slain, to receive power and wealth and wisdom and strength and honor and glory and praise!" (5:12 NIV)

Every creature in heaven, on earth, under the earth, and in the sea sing:
"To him who sits on the throne and to the Lamb be praise and honor and glory and power for ever and ever!" (5:13 NIV)

A great innumerable multitude from every nation shout with a loud voice:
> *"Salvation belongs to our God, who sits on the throne, and to the Lamb." (7:10 NIV)*

The angels before the throne fall on their faces in worship to Almighty God, saying:
> *"Amen! Praise and glory and wisdom and thanks and honor and power and strength be to our God for ever and ever. Amen!" (7:12 NIV)*

The 144,000 sealed and redeemed Israelites sing a new song before the throne to the accompaniment of harps. Only they know the song, as it was not recorded. (14:3)

Those who were victorious over the beast, his image and number, with harps in their hands, sing this song of Moses and of the Lamb:
> *"Great and marvelous are your deeds, Lord God Almighty. Just and true are your ways, King of the ages. Who will not fear you, O Lord, and bring glory to your name? For you alone are holy. All nations will come and worship before you, for your righteous acts have been revealed." (15:3-4 NIV)*

A great multitude in heaven shout:
> *"Hallelujah! Salvation and glory and power belong to our God, for true and just are his judgments..." "Hallelujah!" (19:1-3 NIV)*

And the twenty-four elders and four living creatures fall down and worship God, crying out:
> *"Amen. Hallelujah!" (19:4 NIV)*

What Will We Do?

A voice from the throne rings out with these words:
"Praise our God, all you his servants, you who fear him, both small and great!" *(19:5 NIV)*

A great multitude shouts:
"Hallelujah! For our Lord God Almighty reigns. Let us rejoice and be glad and give him glory! For the wedding of the Lamb has come, and his bride has made herself ready. Fine linen, bright and clean, was given her to wear." *(19:6-8 NIV)*

Eight of these great anthems of praise are spoken. Five are sung. Join in with this heavenly chorus and lift your heart in praise and adoration to the great God Almighty and the Lamb.

We will eat and drink.

What about food in the New Jerusalem? Will we be able to eat and drink in our glorified bodies? This is a very important point to some people. And I must say that most, if not all of us, enjoy a delicious dinner. Food is a major part of our life here on earth, and is absolutely necessary to sustain life. But will it be needed or even possible in the New Jerusalem? Let's take a look at *Revelation 22:1-2* first.

"He then showed me the river of the water of life, as clear as crystal, flowing forth from the throne of God and of the Lamb, and running through the middle of the street, and on this side and that side of the river, the tree of life, bearing twelve kinds of fruit, yielding its fruit every month. And the leaves of the tree are for the healing of the nations." *(ML)*

The river of the Water of Life which flows from the throne of God will flow down the center of the wide street or boulevard with both its banks covered with trees, the Tree of Life. Every month these trees will produce a harvest of fruit, possibly a different kind each month for twelve months. Either that or each harvest will be of 12 different types of fruit. At any rate we know that there will be twelve varieties of fruit on the Tree of Life. No more delicious fruit will ever be ours to enjoy. We will be vegetarians at that time, or should I say "fruitaterians". It will be like the picture that is given to us in *Exodus 24:9-11*. This may surprise you.

"Moses and Aaron, Nadab and Abihu, and the seventy elders of Israel went up and saw the God of Israel. Under his feet was something like a pavement made of sapphire, clear as the sky itself. But God did not raise his hand against these leaders of the Israelites; they saw God, and they ate and drank." (NIV)

Moses and his companions lingered in the very presence of God, standing on what looked like a pavement of crystal clear sapphire. There they ate and drank before God. Where did they get the food? Did they have a picnic lunch with them, and excuse themselves for a little, while they enjoyed their lunch. Not at all! God fed them. He gave them food and water. Just what it was, we have no idea. Heavenly manna? Food from the Tree of Life? What does it matter? The important thing is that they ate and drank before God, evidently of food that He provided.

You remember the Tree of Life from the book of Genesis and the Garden of Eden. Adam and Eve were allowed to eat of its fruit until they sinned by disobeying God by eating from the Tree of the Knowledge

What Will We Do?

of Good and Evil. Were these two the only fruit trees in the garden? Certainly not. God had planted many other fruit trees in the garden also. Let's look at this.

"And out of the ground the Lord God caused to grow every tree that is pleasing to the sight and good for food." (Genesis 2:9a NAS)

"And the Lord God commanded the man, saying, 'From any tree of the garden you may eat freely.'" (Genesis 2:16 NAS)

The Garden of Eden produced every variety of fruit: apples, pears, peaches, mangos, etc. Sure, why not? And if not, where did these fruit trees come from? We sometimes forget that the beginners of the human race were allowed to eat, not only from the Tree of Life, but also from all the other fruit trees, so that they had a great variety of fruit to enjoy. Since there was other fruit in that beautiful garden besides that of the Tree of Life, can it be that there will also be other trees in the New Jerusalem, whose fruit we will enjoy? This could include what we now classify as vegetables. Since it is probably true that our glorified bodies will not need food to sustain them, the fruit that God provides for us in that day will be for our enjoyment. A similar condition will be in vogue during the millennium. In the vision that God gave Ezekiel, he mentions that the water flowing from the temple formed a great river, and then adds:

"And by the river on its banks, on one side and on the other, will grow all kinds of trees for food. Their leaves will not wither and their fruit will not fail. They will bear every month because their water flows from the sanctuary, and their fruit will be for food and their leaves for healing." (Ezekiel 47:12 NAS)

This is a millennial picture. Just like He provided fruit for Adam and Eve, so God will provide fruit for the saved of that 1,000 year period. And so we extend that on to eternity, and can easily believe that, yes, we will eat in the New Jerusalem, fruits and vegetables of all kinds. Those of you who can't live without a delicious steak every now and then will have your tastes changed. Nothing will die in that eternal life-giving time.

You may be puzzled as to why the "leaves of the tree will be for the healing of the nations." If there is no more sickness in our glorified bodies, what need will we have for healing? What need will the nations that surround the celestial city have for healing? The Greek word for healing is the word "therapeian". We get the word "therapy" from this word. It refers to health, general physical well-being. Change the word "healing" to "health". The nations will be healthy. All will enjoy perfect health. The leaves of the trees will contribute to this experience of well-being. Just how, we do not know. Will the leaves be chewed? Will they fall into the river, from which the nations will drink, and thus contribute to the health and well-being of the people? Trees are very important today to provide the oxygen that we breath. Will we also need to breathe in oxygen with our glorified bodies to contribute to our health? I'll tell you when we get there.

We will rest.

One of the seven beatitudes in the book of Revelation promises rest to those who die in the Lord. It is found in chapter 14, verse 13.

"And I heard a voice from heaven, saying, 'Write this: Blessed are the dead who die in the

Lord henceforth.' 'Blessed indeed', says the Spirit, 'that they may rest from their labors, for their deeds follow them.'" (RSV)

Our Savior, the Lord Jesus Christ, offered rest to all who are weary. He invited all such to go to Him.

"Come to Me, all who are weary and heavy-laden, and I will give you rest. Take My yoke upon you, and learn from Me, for I am gentle and humble in heart; and you shall find rest for your souls." (Matthew 11:28-29 NAS)

From what will we rest? We will rest from all our labors and troubles here on earth, from the problems and trials that we faced, from the constant attacks of our enemy Satan, and from all the evil, sin, and sickness of our present earthly existence. And then in the New Jerusalem and renovated earth, since our work will involve serving God and ruling over the nations, it may be that we will have times of rest from this. Will our glorified bodies have need of rest? Don't forget that even God rested on the seventh day from all His work of creation. He did not need rest to revitalize his energy, like we do at the present, yet He did rest. Perhaps the reason was to show us mortals that we need to take times of rest. Even preachers need to take time for restful vacations. I love the poem written by some gifted but unknown author, entitled

The Preacher's Vacation

The old man went to the meetin' for the day was bright and fair,
Though his limbs were very totterin' and t'was hard to travel there.
But he hungered for the Gospel, so he trudged the weary way,
On the road so rough and dusty, 'neath the summer's burnin' ray.

By an by he reached the building, to his soul a holy place;
Then he paused and wiped the sweat drops off his thin and wrinkled face.
But he looked around bewildered for the old bell did not toll;
And the doors were shut and bolted, and he did not see a soul.

So he leaned upon his crutches, and he said, "What does it mean?"
And he looked this way and that way 'till it seemed almost a dream.
He had walked the dusty highways, and he breathed a heavy sigh,
Just to go once more to meetin' ere the summons came to die.
But he saw a little notice tacked upon the meetin' door;
So he limped along to read it, and he read it o'er and o'er.
Then he wiped his dusty glasses, and he read it o'er again
'Till his hands began to tremble and his eyes began to pain.

As the old man read the notice, how it made his spirit burn;
"Pastor absent, on vacation; church is closed 'till his return."
Then he staggered slowly backward and he set him down to think,
For his soul was stirred within him, 'till he thought his heart would sink.

So he mused along and wondered, to himself soliloquized -
"I have lived to almost eighty and was never so surprised,
As I read the oddest notice stickin' to the meetin' door,
'Pastor off on a vacation' - never heard the likes before.

"Why when I first j'ined the meetin' very many years ago,
Preacher traveled on the circuits in the heat and through the snow;
If they got their clothes and vittals, t'was but little cash they got,
They said nothing 'bout vacation, but were happy in their lot.

"Would the farmer leave his cattle, or the shepherd leave his sheep?
Who would give them care and shelter, or provide them food to
eat? So it strikes me very sing'lar when a man of holy hands
Thinks he has to take vacation, and forsakes his tender lambs.

"Did St. Paul git such a notion? Did a Wesley or a Knox?
Did they in the heat of summer turn away their needy flocks?
Did they shut their meetin' houses just to go and lounge about?
Why, they knew that if they did, Satan certainly would shout.

"Do the taverns close their doors just to take a little rest?
Why t'would be the height of nonsense, for their trade would be distressed.
Did you every know it happen, or hear anybody tell,
Satan takin' a vacation, shuttin' up the doors of Hell?

"And shall preachers of the Gospel pack their trunks and go away,
Leavin' saints and dyin' sinners git along as best they may?
Are the souls of dyin' sinners valued less than sellin' beer?
Or do preachers git tired quicker that the rest of mortals here?

"Why it is, I cannot answer, but my feelin's they are stirred;
Here I've dragged my totterin' footsteps for to hear the Gospel Word.
But the preacher is a travelin' and the meetin' house is closed;
I confess it's very trying, hard indeed to keep composed.

"Tell me, when I tread the valley and go up the shinin' height,
Will I hear no angels singin'? Will I see no gleamin' light?
Will the golden harps be silent? Will I meet no welcome there?
Why, the thought is most distractin' - would be more than I could bear.

"Tell me, when I reach the city over on the other shore;
Will I find a little notice tacked upon the golden door,
Tellin' me, 'mid dreadful silence, right in words that cut and burn -
'Jesus absent, on vacation, heaven closed 'till His return."

The poem is great. I love it. And it contains a lot of truth. It does show us the way lots of people used to think, and perhaps some still think this way. However, lest you think that I am against preachers going on a vacation, forget it. Everyone needs some time off now and then to get the batteries recharged. Even preachers. But without closing the church doors. I would add that whether one takes a vacation or even retires, one never stops serving the Lord. A vacation from one activity may open other doors of witness during the time of rest. Retirement should only be from our vocation, never from our avocation of preaching the Gospel and being a witness for Christ. We don't retire from that while here on earth. But one day we will receive our rest, the eternal rest of the soul. While we are serving the Lord, we will be resting from the many trials of today.

Yes, the New Jerusalem will be a marvelous place, an actual, physical city that is prepared for God's people. I love the words of the Psalmist in **Psalm 16:11**.

> **"You will show me the path of life; In Your presence is fullness of joy; At Your right hand are pleasures forevermore." (NKJ)**

In Conclusion, I'd like to quote *James 5:7-9*, and several other verses that inspire and exhort us to be faithful, to persevere, to be patient until that glorious day dawns and we are with the Lord eternally.

"Be patient, therefore, brethren, until the coming of the Lord. Behold, the farmer waits for the precious produce of the soil, being patient about it, until it gets the early and late rains. You too be patient; strengthen your hearts, for the coming of the Lord is at hand. Do not complain, brethren, against one another, that you yourselves may not be judged; behold; the Judge is standing right at the door." (NAS)

Yes, our Judge is standing right at the door. He is listening to all we say, and watching all we do. He is about to enter. And praise God that He is not only our Judge, but also our Savior and Redeemer. James tells us to be patient and persevere. Hang in there! Don't give up! Someone sent me the following poem from an unknown author about the frog who never gave up. Enjoy it.

Two frogs fell into a can of cream, or so it has been told.
The sides of the can were shiny and steep; the cream was deep and cold.
"Oh, what's the use," said number one. "It's plain no help's around.
Goodbye, my friend; goodbye, sad world," and weeping still he drowned.
But number two, of sterner stuff, dog paddled in surprise,
The while he licked his creamy lips and blinked his creamy eyes.
"I'll swim at least a while," he thought, or so it has been said.
"It really wouldn't help the world, if one more frog were dead."
An hour or more he kicked and swam; not once he stopped to mutter.
Then hopped out from the island he had made of fresh churched butter.

The moral of the poem is "keep kicking"! Persevere. Don't give up! The best is yet to come. One day we'll hop out of this slippery and slimy place with all its dangers and land on God's eternal shore. We'll walk the beautiful street of the New Jerusalem.

Three times in Revelation chapter 20 Jesus promises to come quickly.

"And behold I am coming quickly. Blessed is he who heeds the words of the prophecy of this book." (Revelation 22:7 NAS)

"Behold, I am coming quickly, and My reward is with Me, to render to every man according to what he has done." (Revelation 22:12 NAS)

"Yes, I am coming quickly." (Revelation 22:20 NAS)

Are you, my brother in Christ, awaiting His coming with joy and patience? Are you heeding the warnings and exhortations of this book of Revelation and all of God's holy Word? The apostle John's reaction to these glorious promises sets the example for the right reaction by every child of God. He cried out:

"Amen. Come, Lord Jesus." (Revelation 22:20 NAS)

With this story, I close. A visitor to Italy was walking along a country lane one day, when he came upon a beautiful estate. He stopped by the gate and gazed slowly over the colorful and well-manicured gardens. Just then the gardener appeared and took note of the visitor. Then engaged him in a conversation. The owner was away on business, and the gardener did not know when he would return. "These gardens," exclaimed the stranger, "are so well kept and beautiful that it would appear that you are expecting the owner to return tomorrow." The gardener quickly replied: "Today, sir, today."

"Amen. Come, Lord Jesus."